G STREET

F STREET

E STREET

D STREET

C STREET

MASSACHUSETTS AVENUE

'UM

'ATION

**M**

NORTH CAPITOL STREET

NEW JERSEY AVENUE

PENNSYLVANIA AVENUE

THE CAPITOL

4TH STREET

3RD STREET

MARYLAND AVENUE

AMERICAN
INDIAN
*Opening 2004*

AIR AND SPACE

**M**

'ENFANT
PLAZA

# SMITHSONIAN MUSEUMS
## ON OR NEAR THE NATIONAL MALL

Anacostia Museum and the National Zoo are located
elsewhere in Washington, D.C. The Cooper-Hewitt and
American Indian museums are in New York City.

Library of Congress Cata-
loging-in Publication Data
Smithsonian Institution.
Official guide to the
Smithsonian.
  p.  cm.
ISBN 1-58834-003-1
(alk. paper)
1. Smithsonian Institution—
Guidebooks.  2. Washington
(D.C.)—Guidebooks.  3. New
York (N.Y.)—Guidebooks.
I. Title
Q11 .S3 S664 2002
069′.09753—dc21
2001049283

Printed in Italy, not at
government expense
09 08 07 06 05 04 03
5 4 3 2

The paper used in this publication meets the minimum requirements of the American
National Standard for Perma-
nence of Paper for Printed
Library Materials
Z39.48-1984.

Printed by Eurografica,
Vicenza, Italy
Typeset by Blue Heron
Typesetters, Inc.,
Lawrence, Kansas
Typesetting assistance:
Omar Pasha

Guidebook Staff
Executive editor:
Caroline Newman
Editor: Jane McAllister
Designer: Amber Frid-Jimenez
Production manager:
Martha Sewall
Production assistant:
Matt Crosby

The following are among the
many individuals who provided
invaluable assistance in the
preparation of this edition:
Laura Baptiste, Rebecca
Barker, Nancy Bechtol, Bill
Bloomer, Toni Brady, Laura
Brouse-Long, Harold Closter,
Joyce Connolly, Tim Cronen,
Linda Deck, Dru Dowdy,
Jane Gardner, Margie Gibson,
Valeska Hilbig, Jo Hinkel,
Bob Hoage, Elizabeth Johnson,
Sarah King, Barbara Kram,
Sidney Lawrence, Leonda
Levchuk, Kathy Lindeman,
Mary Ann Livingston, Melinda
Machado, Carolyn Margolis,
Kimberly Mayfield, Joan
Mentzer, Helen M. Morrill, Dale
Mott, Catherine Perge, Nancy
Pope, Susan Post, Mary Grace
Potter, Elizabeth Punsalan,
Betsy Robinson, David
Romanowski, Savannah
Schroll, Jo Ann Sims, Lou
Stancari, Frances Stevenson,
Joseph Suarez, Thomas
Sweeney, Maureen Turman,
Michelle Urie, Amy Wilkins,
Emily Winetz, Susan Yelavich.

Photo Credits
David Aaronson, Ernest
Amoroso, Mark Avino, Toni
Brady, Chip Clark, Jessie
Cohen, Dennis Cowley, Harold
Dorwin, Matt Flynn, Katherine
Fogden, Gina Fuentes-Walker,
Andrew Garn, Carmelo
Guadagno, Marianne Gurley,
Bart Kasten, Franko Khoury,
Robert Lautman, Eric Long,
Bruce Miller, James O'Donnell,
Ken Pelka, Dane A. Penland,
Charles H. Phillips, John
Polman, Dean Powell, Carolyn
Russo, Victor Schrager,
Francie Schroeder, Frank G.
Speck, Lee Stalsworth,
Richard Strauss, Steve Tague,
Hugh Talman, Mark Thiessen,
Jeff Tinsley, John Tsantes,
Rick Vargas, John White,
Rolland White, Roger
Whiteside, Gene Young.

Cover: *Portal Gates* by Albert
Paley (American, b. 1944),
1974. Renwick Gallery.

Endsheets: Map of
the National Mall by
Amber Frid-Jimenez
with special assistance
from National Capital
Planning Commission

# CONTENTS

Welcome to the Smithsonian     5

Visiting the Smithsonian in Washington, D.C.     9

About the Smithsonian     17

Especially for Children     32

## SMITHSONIAN MUSEUMS

### ON OR NEAR THE NATIONAL MALL

National Air and Space Museum     37

National Museum of Natural History     67

National Museum of American History,
    Behring Center     95

Freer Gallery of Art     121

Arthur M. Sackler Gallery     127

National Museum of African Art     133

Arts and Industries Building     139

Hirshhorn Museum and Sculpture Garden     143

National Portrait Gallery     153

Smithsonian American Art Museum     161

Renwick Gallery of the Smithsonian
    American Art Museum     169

National Postal Museum     175

### ELSEWHERE IN WASHINGTON, D.C.

Anacostia Museum and Center for
    African American History and Culture     183

National Zoological Park     187

### IN NEW YORK CITY

Cooper-Hewitt, National Design Museum     199

National Museum of the American Indian,
    George Gustav Heye Center     207

Smithsonian across America     217

Smithsonian Institution Memberships     222

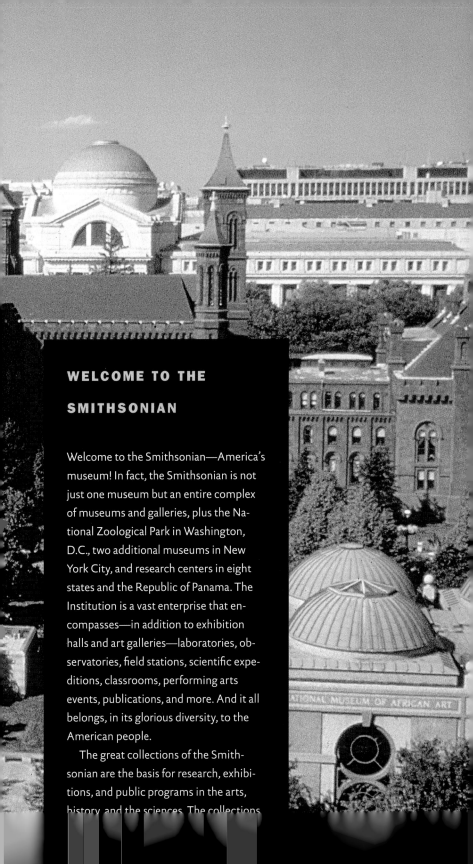

## WELCOME TO THE SMITHSONIAN

Welcome to the Smithsonian—America's museum! In fact, the Smithsonian is not just one museum but an entire complex of museums and galleries, plus the National Zoological Park in Washington, D.C., two additional museums in New York City, and research centers in eight states and the Republic of Panama. The Institution is a vast enterprise that encompasses—in addition to exhibition halls and art galleries—laboratories, observatories, field stations, scientific expeditions, classrooms, performing arts events, publications, and more. And it all belongs, in its glorious diversity, to the American people.

The great collections of the Smithsonian are the basis for research, exhibitions, and public programs in the arts, history, and the sciences. The collections

contain some 142 million objects, ranging from insects and diamonds to locomotives and spacecraft. Indeed, the holdings are so vast that fewer than 2 percent of them are on display at any one time. That's a circumstance we hope to change in the years ahead by rescuing many objects from the limbo of storage and placing them in museums around the country.

The Smithsonian is a monument to the curiosity of Americans—about the world and, especially, about themselves. Smithsonian exhibitions will tell you about the earth and the oceans and all the forms of life they sustain. They'll tell you about the universe, too, and about many countries and cultures. But most of all, they'll tell you the story of America and the mosaic that is our national identity. Through its collections, the Smithsonian presents the astonishing record of American historical, cultural, and scientific achievement with a scope and depth no other institution in the world can match.

In the pages that follow, you'll find many treasures of the Institution pictured and described. But there are many, many more that cannot be included in this guidebook and that await discovery. I urge you to come back often to experience the Smithsonian and to find your own favorite objects, exhibitions, and spaces.

The coming years offer exciting changes at the Smithsonian. Portions of the collections that were previously unavailable to the public will be exhibited, and many of the traditional exhibitions will be reimagined and refreshed. All the familiar objects visitors have loved for decades—from the Star-Spangled Banner to starships—will be newly presented in ways that will make the experience of them wondrous and exciting all over again.

We'll also be sprucing up the museums. The National Portrait Gallery and the Smithsonian American Art Museum, which share space in the Old Patent Office Building in downtown Washington, are being renovated to bring the infrastructure of that magnificent 19th-century landmark up to contempo-

rary standards. While the two museums are closed, portions of the collections are on tour throughout the United States.

We'll also be opening entirely new museums. In December 2003, the National Air and Space Museum will open its spectacular new Steven F. Udvar-Hazy Center on a 176-acre plot near Dulles Airport. So large will the structure be, it could fit the Air and Space building right inside it. The Udvar-Hazy Center will ultimately display nearly 200 aircraft and more than 100 spacecraft (including a space shuttle), and thousands of other significant artifacts related to the history of aviation and spaceflight. The National Museum of the American Indian, being built on the National Mall adjacent to the National Air and Space Museum, is scheduled for completion in the fall of 2004.

So come back often to explore the evolving Smithsonian. And let us know what pleased you about your experience at the Institution—about our buildings and exhibitions and museum stores and cafeterias—and what did not. Our hope is for the Smithsonian to continue all the best traditions of its past while using the technology and design skills of the 21st century to educate and delight our visitors more fully than ever before. Our goal is nothing less than to have the Smithsonian set the standard of museum-going excellence for the world.

Enjoy your visit!

Lawrence M. Small
*Secretary*
*Smithsonian Institution*

**Above and preceding pages: Entrance to the Castle on the south side, from Independence Avenue and the Enid A. Haupt Garden. Overleaf: The serpentine walkways are an integral part of the Mary Livingston Ripley Garden, located along the east side of the Arts and Industries Building.**

Metrorail:
Smithsonian station.
For information about
the Smithsonian, call
202-357-2700 (voice)
or 202-357-1729 (TTY).
For daily 24-hour
recorded information,
call Dial-a-Museum,
202-357-2020
(English);
202-633-9126
(Spanish).
info@si.edu
www.si.edu

# VISITING THE SMITHSONIAN IN WASHINGTON, D.C.

Begin your
Smithsonian visit
at the Smithsonian
Information Center
in the Smithsonian
Institution Building
(the Castle) on
the National Mall,
open daily, except
December 25, from
9 A.M. to 5:30 P.M.

The Smithsonian Institution is a complex
of 16 museums, the National Zoological
Park, and numerous research facilities.
Fourteen museums and the Zoo are
located in Washington, D.C. The Cooper-
Hewitt, National Design Museum and the
National Museum of the American
Indian, George Gustav Heye Center are
in New York City.

Here is some basic information to help
you plan your Smithsonian visit.

## ADMISSION

Admission to all Washington
Smithsonian museums, the National Zoo,
and the National Museum of the American Indian, George Gustav Heye Center in
New York is free.

Above: Edward Hopper
(1882–1967), *Cape Cod
Morning*, oil, 1950.
Smithsonian American
Art Museum. Below:
*Portrait of Yinti, Prince
Xun, and Wife*, hanging
scroll, ink and color on
silk, China, Qing dynasty,
2d half 18th century.
Arthur M. Sackler Gallery.

## HOURS

**Most Smithsonian museums are open
daily, except December 25, from 10 A.M.
to 5:30 P.M.** (check museum listings in
this guide). Extended summer hours are
determined each year. Note the following schedule for the Zoo: May 1–
September 15: grounds are open from
6 A.M. to 8 P.M. and buildings from 10 A.M.
to 6 P.M. (unless otherwise posted);
September 16–April 30: grounds are open from 6 A.M.
to 6 P.M. and buildings from 10 A.M. to 4:30 P.M. (unless
otherwise posted).

## HOW TO GET THERE

We recommend using public transportation, including
taxis, when visiting Washington's attractions. Metrorail, Washington's subway system, and Metrobus link
the downtown area with nearby communities in Maryland and Virginia. To locate the Metrorail station near-
est the museum you wish to visit, see the individual
museum entries in this guide. For more information,
call Metro at 202-637-7000 (voice) or 202-638-3780
(TTY), or visit the Web site wmata.com.

The Smithsonian does not operate public parking
facilities. Limited restricted street parking is available

on and around the National Mall; posted
times are enforced. Some commercial
parking can be found in the area.

## SMITHSONIAN
## INFORMATION CENTER

Open daily at 9 A.M. in the Castle, the
Smithsonian Information Center offers
visitors a multifaceted information and
orientation program, with volunteer
information specialists on duty to
answer questions and give directions
until 4 P.M. A free general brochure is

available in various languages. Write or call:
Smithsonian Information, Smithsonian Institution,
SI Building, Room 153, Washington, D.C. 20560-0010;
**202-357-2700 (voice); 202-357-1729 (TTY).** For daily 24-
hour recorded information about Smithsonian activities, call Dial-a-Museum: 202-357-2020 (English);
202-633-9126 (Spanish). E-mail: info@si.edu.

## ACCESSIBILITY
*Smithsonian Access,* a free guide for
visitors with disabilities, is available
on request. See above for information on how to obtain a copy.

## ON-LINE INFORMATION
A wealth of information about the
Smithsonian and its resources is
available on-line at www.si.edu.

M. F. K. Fisher
(1908–1992) by Ginny
Stanford (b. 1950),
acrylic on canvas, 1991.
National Portrait Gallery.
© Ginny Stanford.

## PHOTOGRAPHY
Video cameras are permitted for personal use in most
museums. Photography is permitted in permanent-
collection exhibitions but is generally prohibited in
special, temporary exhibitions. The use of flash
attachments and tripods is prohibited in all buildings.
Exceptions to these rules may occur in any exhibition or
building. Ask at the information desk at the museum you
are visiting for specific guidelines about photography.

## PETS
With the exception of service animals, pets are not
permitted in any of the museums or at the Zoo.

## SMOKING
Smoking is prohibited in all Smithsonian facilities.

## WHERE TO EAT
Food service is available in the National Air and Space
Museum; the National Museum of American History,

Behring Center; and the National Museum of Natural History. An outdoor café is open during the summer at the Hirshhorn Museum and Sculpture Garden. Beverage and snack service is available in the Arts and Industries Building. The Castle offers luncheon service Mondays through Saturdays and on holidays, and brunch on Sundays. The Zoo has a variety of fast-food services.

## MUSEUM STORES
Located in most Smithsonian museums, the stores carry books, crafts, graphics, jewelry, reproductions, toys, and gifts that relate to the museums' collections. The Arts and Industries Building store also features Smithsonian mail-order catalogue items.

## SIGHTSEEING TOURS

Tourmobile, the only commercial sightseeing service federally authorized to operate on the National Mall, offers narrated tours with stops at Smithsonian museums, major memorials and monuments, government and historic buildings, and Arlington National Cemetery. Fees include reboarding options. Information is subject to change. Call 202-554-5100 (recording) or visit the Web site tourmobile.com.

**Above: Frieze, gray-blue slate, Pakistan, Kushan dynasty (A.D. 50–200), late 2d–early 3d century A.D. Freer Gallery of Art.**

**The National Mall has traditionally been the setting for large-scale events in the nation's capital.**

## THE NATIONAL MALL

A long, open, grassy stretch from the Capitol to the Washington Monument, the original National Mall was an important feature of Pierre L'Enfant's 1791 plan for the city of Washington. He envisioned it as a "vast esplanade" lined with grand residences. Before the Smithsonian Institution Building (the Castle) was built in the mid-19th century, however, the National Mall was used mainly for grazing and gardens. To the west, beyond the spot where the Washington Monument now stands, were tidal flats and marshes. After those areas were gradually filled, the National Mall was officially extended in the 20th century to the Lincoln Memorial.

In 1850, New York horticulturist Andrew Jackson Downing was commissioned to landscape the National

Mall. But his design, which called for curving carriage drives amid a grove of American evergreens, was only partly realized. By 1900, the National Mall had deteriorated. Its eyesores included a railroad station with sheds, tracks, and coal piles. Two years later, work was begun to implement L'Enfant's early concept. Over the years, much of his vision has become reality on a National Mall lined by rows of great museum buildings.

On the National Mall today, people jog, fly kites, toss Frisbees, or just stroll. Near the Castle, children ride on an old-fashioned carousel. For a time each summer, the colorful Smithsonian Folklife Festival fills the National Mall with traditional music and crafts. On the benches alongside the walkways, visitors rest while deciding which Smithsonian museum to explore next.

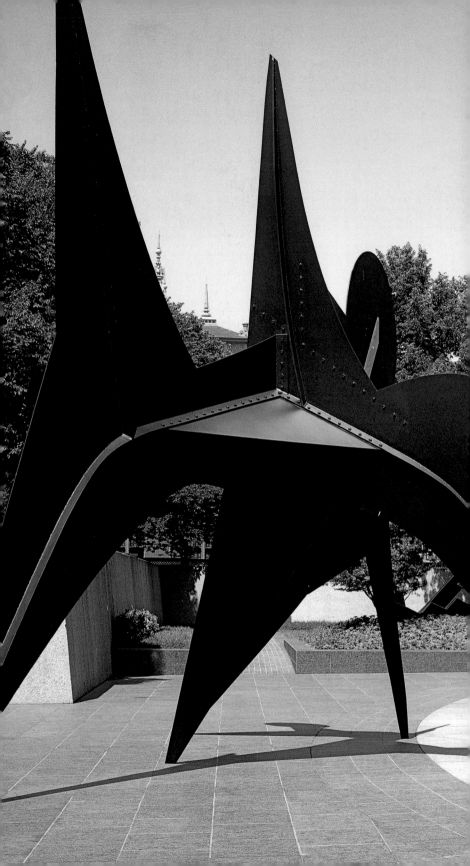

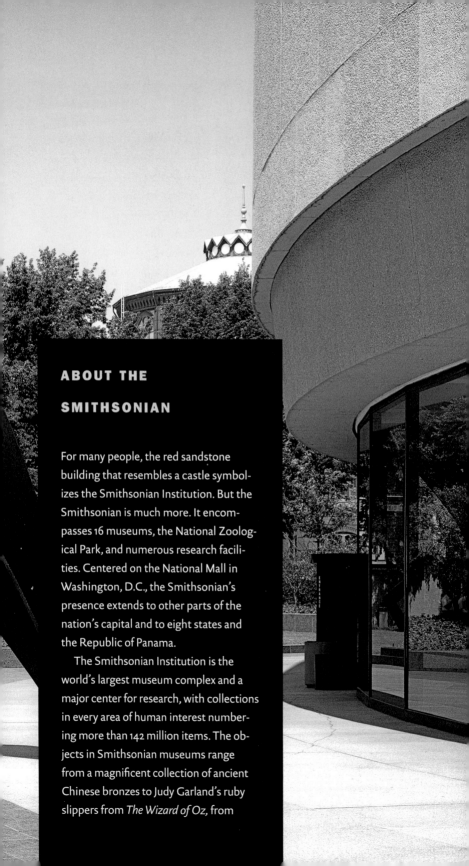

## ABOUT THE

## SMITHSONIAN

For many people, the red sandstone building that resembles a castle symbolizes the Smithsonian Institution. But the Smithsonian is much more. It encompasses 16 museums, the National Zoological Park, and numerous research facilities. Centered on the National Mall in Washington, D.C., the Smithsonian's presence extends to other parts of the nation's capital and to eight states and the Republic of Panama.

The Smithsonian Institution is the world's largest museum complex and a major center for research, with collections in every area of human interest numbering more than 142 million items. The objects in Smithsonian museums range from a magnificent collection of ancient Chinese bronzes to Judy Garland's ruby slippers from *The Wizard of Oz*, from

Above: Willem de Kooning (American, b. Rotterdam, The Netherlands, 1904–1997), *Woman, Sag Harbor*, 1964, oil and charcoal on wood. Hirshhorn Museum and Sculpture Garden. Preceding pages: *Two Discs*, 1965, a "stabile" by Alexander Calder (American, 1898–1976), stands at the entrance to the Hirshhorn Museum.

memorabilia of the U.S. presidency to the Apollo lunar landing module to a 3.5-billion-year-old fossil. The scope is staggering. All of these objects help us understand the past, consider the present, and preserve history for future generations.

Only a small part of the Smithsonian's collections is on display in the museums at any one time. Scholars and scientists use the rest behind the scenes as they work to increase our knowledge of science, art, and history. On expeditions to all parts of the world, Smithsonian scientists regularly gather new facts and specimens. Smithsonian exhibitions, scholarly publications, and Web sites make available much of the information that the experts assemble.

## A CENTER FOR LEARNING

The Smithsonian is deeply involved in public education for people of all ages. Visiting groups of school-children are a common sight in the museums, and families come together here on weekend outings and summer vacations. Educators from the elementary school through the university level use the Smithsonian's resources, as do scholars pursuing advanced research. Through The Smithsonian Associates, adults and children enjoy classes, lectures, studio arts courses, and a variety of other educational activities.

The Smithsonian also offers an exciting schedule of "living exhibits." Performing-arts activities include music, theater, dance, film programs, and Discovery Theater performances for youngsters. Important behind-the-scenes resources include the Smithsonian Center for Latino Initiatives (latino.si.edu), which sup-

ports exhibitions, research, and educational initiatives that illuminate and highlight Latino contributions to America and permit a wider sharing of Latino accomplishments in the sciences, humanities, and performing arts. The Smithsonian Asian Pacific American Program (www.apa.si.edu) inspires a broad understanding of our nation and its many cultures by tracing and interpreting the contributions of Asian Pacific Americans in the United States. The National Science Resources Center (www.si.edu/nsrc), operated jointly by the Smithsonian and The National Academies, works to improve the quality of science education in the nation's elementary and secondary schools.

**The National Air and Space Museum with the Capitol in the background.**

The popular Smithsonian Folklife Festival, a celebration of the nation's and the world's rich cultural heritage, brings musicians and craftspeople to the National Mall each summer. Held outdoors for approximately two weeks every summer, the festival educates a broad public about diverse cultural heritages and encourages tradition bearers by giving recognition to their artistry, knowledge, and wisdom.

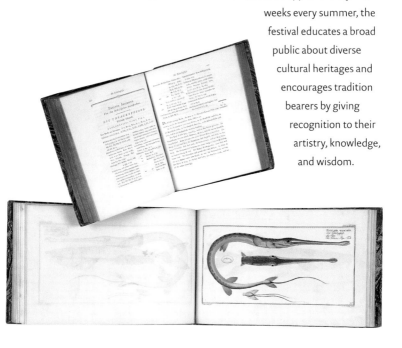

**Marcus Elieser Bloch (1723–1799),** *Allgemeine Naturgeschichte der Fischee* **(General Natural History of Fishes), 1782–95. Smithsonian Institution Libraries.**

### SMITHSONIAN INSTITUTION LIBRARIES

This 22-branch library system boasts collections of 1.5 million volumes, of which 40,000 are rare books. Smithsonian Institution Libraries holdings also include a unique and distinguished collection of manufacturers' trade literature (285,000 pieces representing 30,000 companies) and World's Fair materials. Branch libraries can be visited by appointment only. Digital exhibitions and digitized editions of rare books are on view at www.sil.si.edu. (For information about the Smithsonian Institution Libraries Gallery, see the entry on the National Museum of American History, Behring Center in this guide.)

### NATIONAL OUTREACH

As a national institution, the Smithsonian takes cultural and educational programs to people across the country.

The Smithsonian Associates sponsors lectures, tours, and other events nationwide. Smithsonian Affiliations is an innovative, collections-based initiative that shares Smithsonian collections, staff expertise, and programmatic resources with communities across the United States. The Smithsonian Center for Education and

**Each spring, kite flyers from around the world take part in The Smithsonian Associates' Kite Festival on the National Mall.**

**Mapuche poncho, early
20th century, Chile.
Mrs. Thea Heye-Lothrop
Expedition. National
Museum of the American
Indian.**

Museum Studies provides programs for classrooms and learning opportunities for teachers and students across the nation. The Smithsonian Institution Traveling Exhibition Service develops and circulates exhibitions to many communities. (For more information on these national programs, see "Smithsonian across America" at the back of this guide.) Smithsonian publications make available the expertise that its scholars assemble. *Smithsonian* and *Air & Space/Smithsonian* magazines publish lively articles on topics inspired by Smithsonian activities. Through the World Wide Web, home and school computer users have instant access to a rich resource with which to plan a visit, conduct research, find out about programs and exhibitions, and communicate with the Smithsonian.

## RESEARCH AT THE SMITHSONIAN

The Smithsonian is a preeminent research center. Its research activities are known throughout the world for their benefit to the scholarly community and to the advancement of knowledge. Smithsonian scientists, historians, and art historians explore topics as diverse as global environmental concerns, the nature of the world's changing human and social systems, and the care and preservation of museum objects.

### ARCHIVES OF AMERICAN ART

The Archives collects and preserves materials documenting the history of the visual arts in the United States. Headquartered in Washington, D.C., the Archives also

has regional centers in New York City and San Marino, California. For information, call 202-275-2156.

## SMITHSONIAN CENTER FOR MATERIALS RESEARCH AND EDUCATION

Scientists and conservators at this laboratory, located at the Smithsonian's Museum Support Center in Suitland, Maryland, use the latest technology to carry out research in the technical study, analysis, and conservation of art and archaeological objects. Its education and outreach programs offer exhibitions, specialized courses, and reference services as well as collaboration with educational institutions. The center is open to the public by appointment; call 301-238-3700.

## CONSERVATION AND RESEARCH CENTER, NATIONAL ZOOLOGICAL PARK

This 3,100-acre wooded area in the foothills of the Blue Ridge Mountains in Front Royal, Virginia, is a breeding preserve and study center for rare and endangered animals. It is not open to the public.

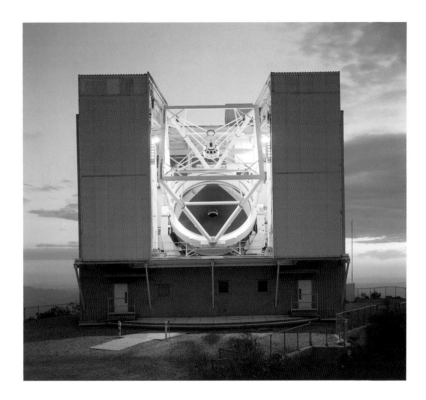

**The Smithsonian Astro-physical Observatory's multiple-mirror telescope glows against the Arizona sunset.**

## SMITHSONIAN MARINE STATION AT FORT PIERCE

Smithsonian Marine Station scientists specialize in marine biodiversity and ecosystems of south Florida. Research focuses on the Indian River Lagoon and the offshore waters of Florida's east central coast, with comparative studies throughout coastal Florida. The station is a research facility of the National Museum of Natural History. For information, call 561-465-6630.

## SMITHSONIAN ASTROPHYSICAL OBSERVATORY

This research center is part of the Harvard-Smithsonian Center for Astrophysics in Cambridge, Massachusetts. Smithsonian Astrophysical Observatory scientists—international leaders in theoretical astrophysics, ground-based gamma-ray astronomy, and stellar atmospheres—study the physical characteristics and evolution of the Universe. The Smithsonian Astrophysical Observatory also has facilities in Amado, Arizona, and Mauna Kea, Hawaii. The largest field facility is the Fred Lawrence Whipple Observatory on Mount Hopkins near Tucson, Arizona. For information about public programs, visit cfa-www.harvard.edu or call the Public Affairs Office in Cambridge at 617-495-7461 or the Whipple Observatory at 602-670-5707.

## SMITHSONIAN ENVIRONMENTAL RESEARCH CENTER

Scientists and visiting researchers at the 3,000-acre site on the shores of the Chesapeake Bay, located seven miles south of Annapolis, Maryland, study land-water relationships and determine how they are affected by human disturbance. Staff conduct public education programs that disseminate the center's research and increase awareness of ecosystems, such as forests, wetlands, and estuaries. Distance Learning programs are available; call 301-261-3204 or visit www.serc.si.edu/education. For information about public programs, call 443-482-2216 or e-mail education@serc.si.edu.

## SMITHSONIAN TROPICAL RESEARCH INSTITUTE

Scientists from the Smithsonian and all over the world study the evolution and behavior of tropical organisms at various facilities of this institute in the Republic of Panama. For information, call 011-507-212-8000.

## HISTORY OF THE SMITHSONIAN

The Smithsonian owes its origin to James Smithson, a British scientist who never visited the United States. Smithson named his nephew Henry James Hungerford as the beneficiary in his will. He stipulated that should Hungerford die without heirs (as he did in 1835), the entire Smithson fortune would go to this country. The purpose would be to found "at Washington, under the

**The Smithsonian Tropical Research Institute pioneered the use of construction cranes for research in the upper forest canopy.**

name of the Smithsonian Institution, an establishment for the increase and diffusion of knowledge."

On July 1, 1836, Congress accepted Smithson's legacy and pledged the faith of the United States to the charitable trust. In 1838, after British courts had approved the bequest, the nation received Smithson's estate—bags of gold sovereigns, then the equivalent of more than a half-million dollars, a great fortune in those days. Eight years later, on August 10, 1846, President James K. Polk signed an Act of Congress establishing the Smithsonian Institution in its present form and providing for the administration of the Smithson trust, independent of the government itself, by a Board of Regents and Secretary of the Smithsonian.

With the formal creation of the Smithsonian came a commitment to the work that continues today in research, museum and library operation, and the dissemination of information in the fields of science, art, and history.

Today, the Smithsonian is a national institution that receives a substantial appropriation from the federal government. Essential funding also comes from private sources, including the Smithson trust, other endowments, individuals, foundations, corporations, and revenues raised from such activities as membership programs, a mail-order catalogue, museum stores, food services, and the Smithsonian Institution Press.

**A statue of Joseph Henry, first Secretary of the Smithsonian, enjoys a prominent setting at the Castle's entrance on the National Mall.**

The chief executive officer of the Smithsonian is the Secretary. The Institution is governed by a Board of Regents, which by law is composed of the vice president of the United States, the chief justice of the United States, three members of the Senate, three members of the House of Representatives, and nine private citizens. The chief justice has traditionally served as chancellor of the Smithsonian.

Each museum has its own director and staff. The central administration of the Smithsonian is headquartered in the Castle building.

## THE CASTLE

The Smithsonian Institution Building, popularly known as the Castle, was designed in Norman style (a 12th-century combination of late Romanesque and early Gothic motifs) by James Renwick Jr., architect of Grace Church and St. Patrick's Cathedral in New York and the Renwick Gallery of the Smithsonian American Art Museum in Washington.

A disastrous fire in 1865—just 10 years after the Castle was completed—caused extensive damage and the loss of valuable objects. Restoration of the building took two years. In the 1880s, much of the Castle was remodeled and enlarged.

The Castle originally housed the entire Smithsonian, which included a science museum, lecture hall, art gallery, research laboratories, administrative offices, and living quarters for the Secretary and his family. Today, administrative offices and the Smithsonian Information Center are located here.

**The Smithsonian Institution Building, known as the Castle, was designed by architect James Renwick Jr. and completed in 1855.**

The Smithsonian Information Center opens daily
(except December 25) at 9 A.M.

## ENID A. HAUPT GARDEN AND
## S. DILLON RIPLEY CENTER

Behind the Castle is a magnificent parklike garden
named for its donor, philanthropist Enid Annenberg
Haupt. Changing with the seasons, it features
exquisite trees, shrubs, and flowers. In the center is a
large 19th-century parterre. Pieces of Victorian garden
furniture, some dating from the early days of the
Castle and the Arts and Industries Building, are placed
throughout the more than four acres of gardens. The
garden opens daily, except December 25,
at 7 A.M.; closing hours are determined
seasonally.

Beneath the Haupt Garden is a three-
level underground museum, research, and
education complex that contains the
Arthur M. Sackler Gallery, the National
Museum of African Art, and the S. Dillon
Ripley Center. The museums are accessible
through aboveground entrance pavilions.
Through a bronze-domed kiosk, visitors
enter the Ripley Center, named for the
Smithsonian's eighth Secretary. It currently
houses the International Gallery with its
changing exhibitions, workshops, and
classrooms for public programs, and a
lecture hall. The Smithsonian Associates and the
Smithsonian Institution Traveling Exhibition Service
have their offices in the Ripley Center.

**The African crowned
crane is one of the most
spectacular birds in the
National Zoo's collection.**

### OTHER SMITHSONIAN GARDENS

The Horticulture Services Division of the Smithsonian
has designed and created many beautiful gardens
around Smithsonian buildings on the National Mall.
From mid-April through September (weather permitting), Smithsonian horticulturists lead 30- to 45-

Top: The central area of the Hirshhorn Museum's Sculpture Garden, with Alexander Calder's *Six Dots over a Mountain*, 1956, in the foreground, near the reflecting pool. Bottom: The Butterfly Habitat Garden.

minute tours. Check at any information desk for information about tours.

At the east end of the Castle, the Kathrine Dulin Folger Rose Garden features roses and other flowering plants that bloom year-round (no tours available). The Mary Livingston Ripley Garden, located between the Arts and Industries Building and the Hirshhorn Museum and Sculpture Garden, features seasonal plantings and a miniature bulb collection. The Butterfly Habitat Garden on the east side of the National Museum of Natural History emphasizes the special interactions between plants and insects, which are described in interpretive signs.

# SMITHSONIAN SECRETARIES: 1846 TO TODAY

**JOSEPH HENRY,** a famous physical scientist and a pioneer and inventor in electricity, was founding Secretary from 1846 until his death in 1878. Henry set the Smithsonian's course with an emphasis on science. **SPENCER FULLERTON BAIRD,** a naturalist, served from 1878 until his death in 1887. Baird developed the early Smithsonian museums and promoted the accumulation of natural history specimens and collections of all kinds. **SAMUEL PIERPONT LANGLEY,** whose particular interests were aeronautics, astrophysics, and astronomy, launched the Smithsonian in those directions during his years in office, from 1887 to 1906. **CHARLES DOOLITTLE WALCOTT,** a geologist and paleontologist, was Secretary from 1907 to 1927. During his administration, the National Museum of Natural History and the Freer Gallery of Art opened to the public, and the National Collection of Fine Arts (now the Smithsonian American Art Museum) became a separate museum of the Smithsonian. **CHARLES GREELEY ABBOT,** Secretary from 1928 to 1944, was a specialist in solar radiation and solar power. He established a bureau to study the effect of light on plant and animal life, the precursor to the Smithsonian Environmental Research Center. **ALEXANDER WETMORE,** an ornithologist, succeeded Abbot in 1945. During his tenure, which ended in 1952, the National Air Museum (now the National Air and Space Museum) and the Canal Biological Area (now the Smithsonian Tropical Research Institute) became part of the Institution. **LEONARD CARMICHAEL,** a physiological psychologist and former Tufts University president, held office between 1953 and 1964. During those years, the National Museum of History and Technology (now the National Museum of American History, Behring Center) opened. **S. DILLON RIPLEY,** biologist, ecologist, and authority on birds of East Asia, served from 1964 to 1984. Under his leadership, the Smithsonian expanded, adding the Hirshhorn Museum and Sculpture Garden, the National Museum of African Art, the Renwick Gallery, and the Cooper-Hewitt Museum (now the Cooper-Hewitt, National Design Museum). The National Air and Space Museum moved to its present building, and construction began on the underground complex for the National Museum of African Art and the Arthur M. Sackler Gallery. Ripley also encouraged innovative ways of serving a wider public. **ROBERT McC. ADAMS,** an anthropologist, archaeologist, and university administrator, served from 1984 to 1994. During his time as Secretary, the Smithsonian placed new emphasis on broader involvement of diverse cultural communities and focused on enhancing research support and education outreach. The National Museum of the American Indian was established as part of the Smithsonian during Adams's administration. **I. MICHAEL HEYMAN,** a law professor and former chancellor of the University of California at Berkeley, was Secretary from 1994 to 1999. During his tenure, the Smithsonian began a program of reaching out to Americans who do not visit Washington, D.C. Initiatives included a first-ever traveling exhibition of treasures for the Institution's 150th anniversary in 1996; a Smithsonian site on the World Wide Web; and the new Affiliations Program for the long-term loan of collections. **LAWRENCE M. SMALL** was president and chief operating officer of Fannie Mae, the world's largest housing finance company, before his installation as the 11th Secretary on January 24, 2000. At the start of the new century, his goal is to modernize the Smithsonian to better serve all Americans wherever they live. Outreach and education programs, especially the Affiliations Program, which shares our nation's treasures with museums across the country, are being expanded. Four major building and renovation projects are under way, as are public and private sector fundraising efforts to support those initiatives. In addition, the Smithsonian continues to explore ways to improve scientific research at the Institution. For more on Secretary Small's plans, see his "Welcome to the Smithsonian" in the front of this guide.

## THINGS TO SEE AND DO AT THE SMITHSONIAN

Before your visit, call Smithsonian Information at 202-357-2700 (voice) or 202-357-1729 (TTY) and ask for "Ten Tips for Visiting the Smithsonian Museums with Children." Or check our Web site, www.si.edu.

### NATIONAL AIR AND SPACE MUSEUM

The National Air and Space Museum offers a range of programs for families, children, and school groups. Tours, lectures, workshops, films, and performances are scheduled throughout the year. Ask at the museum's information desk for a current calendar of events and about events for the day. Children especially enjoy the spectacular IMAX® films on air-and-space–related topics shown on the five-story-high screen in the Langley IMAX® Theater. The Albert Einstein Planetarium features lectures on the night sky and multimedia programs on astronomy and space. Both have admission fees.

### NATIONAL MUSEUM OF NATURAL HISTORY

After marveling at the African Bush elephant, dinosaurs, and the gems and minerals (including the famous Hope Diamond), children can enjoy a variety of participatory activities. In the O. Orkin Insect Zoo, crawl through a model of a termite mound, look into a real beehive, and hold some of the insects in the zoo. Popular tarantula feedings take place several times a day.

The Discovery Room (first floor) is a family-oriented education center where visitors can touch, smell, and taste objects from the world of nature. For hours and other information, see the museum listing in this guide.

The Discovery Center houses the 400-seat Samuel C. Johnson IMAX® Theater, which shows large-format 2-D and 3-D films on a six-story screen, and Immersion Cinema, which allows the audience to interact with the featured fictional show. Both charge admission. Tickets are available in the Discovery Center. Visit www.mnh.si.edu or call 202-633-7400 for more information.

### NATIONAL MUSEUM OF AMERICAN HISTORY, BEHRING CENTER

In the Hands On Science Center (adjacent to the "Science in American Life" exhibition, first floor), children experience the fun and excitement of experimental science. Activities for visitors ages 5 and older include testing for food additives and finding out the ultraviolet rating of their sunglasses.

Touch, examine, and use objects similar to those elsewhere in the museum at the Hands On History Room (second floor). Visitors ages 5 and older can try more than 30 activities. Young children especially enjoy unpacking Betsy's Moving Trunk, which lets them learn about life on a Virginia plantation in the 1780s.

Note: For both the Hands On History Room and Hands On Science Center, children ages 5 to 12 must be accompanied by an adult. Children under 5 are not admitted.

The week before New Year's, the museum often stages a Holiday Celebration, with singing, dancing, baking, and crafts.

## FREER GALLERY OF ART AND ARTHUR M. SACKLER GALLERY

Programs for young visitors include "ImaginAsia," which uses an adult-child self-guided art tour as inspiration for a project that children may create with help from the education staff. Activity guides for some exhibitions also help family groups enjoy the gallery together.

## NATIONAL MUSEUM OF AFRICAN ART

"AfriKid Art" introduces children to traditional African arts and cultures through workshops, storytelling, and other activities. Programs for families are often offered with special exhibitions. Look for the "Images of Power and Identity" family guide.

## HIRSHHORN MUSEUM AND SCULPTURE GARDEN

Children accompanied by adults can explore the Hirshhorn with the museum's *Family Guide* or join "Young at Art" programs on select Saturday mornings for interactive gallery visits and hands-on workshops. Children can also participate with adults in "Improv Art" sessions, a monthly Saturday drop-in art experience, which includes self-guided gallery activity sheets and hands-on projects. The Hirshhorn offers "family fun" days several times throughout the year, which include art activities, music, storytelling, performers outdoors on the Plaza, along with refreshments, treasure hunts, and prizes. An interactive docent-led "Learning to Look" tour for families is offered once a month. A stroll through the Sculpture Garden is another popular family activity.

### NATIONAL PORTRAIT GALLERY

While the Gallery is closed for renovation, children can test their knowledge of American history on-line by matching clues about significant people in the collection with their portraits. To participate, look for "A Brush with History" at the museum's Web site, www.npg.si.edu, and click on "The Great History Mystery."

### SMITHSONIAN AMERICAN ART MUSEUM

The museum, closed for renovation, offers on-line activities at AmericanArt.si.edu for children of all ages. *Kids' Corner* is an interactive art activity room and *¡del Coraz@n!*, is a bilingual Webzine for teachers and students. In conjunction with the virtual exhibition "Panoramas: The North American Landscape in Art," children from across North America can participate in a global classroom. The museum also offers docent-led virtual field trips via on-line sessions and video conferences for schoolchildren across the country, and an virtual

community for children to learn about artist George Catlin and his portrayal of Native Americans.

### RENWICK GALLERY OF THE SMITHSONIAN AMERICAN ART MUSEUM

The Renwick Gallery offers a number of public programs and family days for children of all ages. Activities range from craft demonstrations and gallery talks to hands-on workshops with artists, museum docents, and education specialists. Look for upcoming programs on the museum's Web site, AmericanArt.si.edu.

### NATIONAL POSTAL MUSEUM

The museum is designed for a family audience, with state-of-the-art interactive displays, inviting exhibit design, and activities geared to adults and children. Try some of the 30 audiovisual and interactive areas, the three computer games, and the computer kiosk where you can address, meter, and send personalized postcards. Participatory displays invite you to travel on the first postal road, open a mailbag, or sort the mail. Once a month the Discovery

Center features self-directed family activities and crafts that reflect museum themes; check at the information desk for date and time.

## ANACOSTIA MUSEUM

Exhibition tours are offered to schools throughout the year. Family activities at the museum include music, storytelling, festivals, and events held in conjunction with special exhibitions. Selected outreach programs and summer enrichment programs present a variety of activities on African American history and culture.

## NATIONAL ZOO

A pair of giant pandas, big cats, elephants, great apes, and reptiles are Zoo favorites for children of all ages. To see the pandas Mei Xiang (Beautiful Fragrance) and Tian Tian (More and More) when they are most active, visit early in the day or late in the afternoon. Observe elephants being trained in the Elephant House or outside (weather permitting), or watch a seal and sea lion feeding and training demonstration.

In the Amazonia rainforest exhibition, explore specimens and artifacts in the biologist's field station. The Reptile Discovery Center features hands-on activities and the chance to see endangered Komodo dragons, the world's largest lizards.

"How Do You Zoo?" in the Visitors Center and the Bird Resource Center in the Bird House are good places to discover more about the animals by exploring, looking, touching, and reading. Check for hours of operation at the Visitors Center.

## NATIONAL MUSEUM OF THE AMERICAN INDIAN, GEORGE GUSTAV HEYE CENTER

At the museum in New York City, public programs, such as Talking Circles and the "Native American Expressive Culture" series, introduce children to Native music, dance, media arts, visual arts, theater, storytelling, and lectures. In the Heye Center, adults and children can learn more about the museum—as well as Native life and history—using the latest computer technology.

## CAROUSEL ON THE MALL

For a perfect break from museums for adults and children, take a ride on the carousel on the National Mall near the Arts and Industries Building. It operates daily 11 A.M. to 5 P.M., weather permitting. There is a small fee.

## DISCOVERY THEATER

Located in the Arts and Industries Building, this popular theater for young audiences ages 3 to 14 presents live performances by storytellers, puppeteers, dancers, actors, and singers October through July. For show times, tickets, performance location, and reservations, call 202-357-1500 Monday through Friday.

Above: The Bell X-1 *Glamorous Glennis* cockpit remains much the same as it was when Chuck Yeager first exceeded the speed of sound on October 14, 1947. Opposite top: The Boeing F4B-4 biplane served as the main fighter for the U.S. Navy and Army Air Corps from the late 1920s to the mid-1930s. Opposite bottom: *Continuum,* a cast bronze sculpture by Charles O. Perry, installed in front of the museum's Independence Avenue entrance.

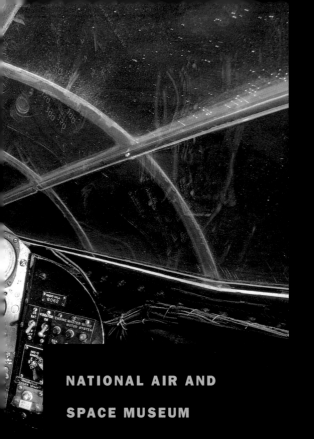

Independence Avenue
at 6th Street, SW.
Mall entrance:
Jefferson Drive at
6th Street, SW.
Open daily, except
December 25,
10 A.M. to 5:30 P.M.
Metrorail: L'Enfant
Plaza station.
Smithsonian
information:
202-357-2700
TTY: 202-357-1729.
www.nasm.si.edu

# NATIONAL AIR AND
# SPACE MUSEUM

Young or old, flight buff or harried tourist,
everyone who has walked through the
National Air and Space Museum has
shared a distinctive and memorable experience. The museum has a vast assemblage
of aircraft, spacecraft, and related artifacts
for visitors to see, but your visit will involve
more than that. The museum is a place
where history is relived, horizons are
expanded, optimism is rekindled, pride is
reborn, and wonder is renewed.

The National Air and Space Museum
tells the story of aeronautics and space
flight in 23 galleries, each devoted to a subject or theme. Visitors are surrounded by
visual excitement—theaters, multimedia
shows, dioramas, interactive computers,
and many innovative exhibits. More than
360 historic or technologically significant
aircraft, about 300 rockets and spacecraft,

Below: The museum's
Viking Lander is similar
to the two that soft-
landed on Mars in 1976
and sent back images
and data from the sur-
face. Opposite: In 1965,
from the Gemini IV
spacecraft, astronaut Ed-
ward White became the
first to "walk" in space.
Crewmate James McDi-
vitt remained in the craft.

and hundreds of engines, propellers, scale models, aviation uniforms, space suits, awards, works of art, instruments, flight equipment, and other items are on display.
About 10 percent of the collection is exhibited at any
one time. Most artifacts are stored at the Paul E. Garber
Preservation, Restoration and Storage Facility, while a
significant number are on loan to other museums.

Nearly all of the aircraft and most of the spacecraft
in the galleries are genuine. Since many spacecraft
cannot be recovered once launched, the museum displays either the backup vehicle, a test vehicle, or a
replica made from authentic hardware, as similar to
the original as possible. Labels note such distinctions.

The logical place to start a tour of the museum is
the Milestones of Flight gallery at the Mall entrance.

## GALLERY 100. Milestones of Flight
*Famous airplanes and spacecraft that are historic
milestones are displayed on two visual levels*

### GROUND LEVEL

**MERCURY *FRIENDSHIP 7*.** First U.S.
manned orbital flight, 1962; piloted
by astronaut John Glenn

**GEMINI IV.** First U.S. space
walk, 1965; space suits
worn by astronauts
Edward H. White II and
James A. McDivitt

**APOLLO 11 COMMAND MODULE
*COLUMBIA*.** First lunar landing mission, 1969; space suit worn by astronaut Michael Collins

**TOUCHABLE MOON ROCK.**
Collected from the lunar surface by Apollo 17 astronauts

**VIKING LANDER.** Test vehicle for the first spacecraft to
operate on the surface of another planet (Mars), 1976

**BREITLING *ORBITER 3* GONDOLA.** From the first
balloon to fly nonstop around the world, 1999

The 1903 Wright Flyer hangs from the ceiling of the Milestones of Flight gallery, which displays aircraft and spacecraft that have made aviation history.

**GODDARD ROCKETS.** Full-scale model of the world's first liquid propellant rocket, 1926, and a larger rocket, 1941

**PERSHING-II (U.S.) AND SS-20 (USSR) MISSILES.** Two disarmed missiles that represent the more than 2,600 nuclear intermediate-range ballistic missiles banned by the Intermediate Nuclear Forces Treaty of 1987

UPPER LEVEL

**1903 WRIGHT FLYER.** Aircraft flown by the Wright brothers at Kitty Hawk, North Carolina, making it the first successful powered, controlled, and sustained flight by humans in a heavier-than-air craft, 1903 (to be moved to Gallery 209 in 2003)

**BELL X-1 *GLAMOROUS GLENNIS*.** First airplane to fly faster than the speed of sound, piloted by Charles E. "Chuck" Yeager, 1947

**RYAN NYP *SPIRIT OF ST. LOUIS*.** Airplane in which Charles Lindbergh made the first nonstop solo transatlantic flight, 1927

**BELL XP-59A AIRACOMET.** First American turbojet aircraft, 1942

**EXPLORER 1.** Backup for the first U.S. satellite to orbit Earth, 1958

**SPUTNIK 1.** Soviet replica of the first artificial satellite to orbit Earth, 1957

**PIONEER 10.** Prototype for the first unmanned spacecraft to fly by Jupiter and Saturn and out of the solar system, launched in 1972

**NORTH AMERICAN X-15.** First piloted aircraft to exceed six times the speed of sound (4,534 miles per hour) and the first to explore the fringes of space, 1967

**MARINER 2.** Backup of the first interplanetary probe to study another planet (Venus), 1962

GALLERY 101. Museum Store

**STAR TREK *ENTERPRISE* MODEL.** Used in filming the television series

**PITTS S-15 SPECIAL.** Small aerobatic biplane designed by Curtis Pitts. It dominated the unlimited class in world-championship competition, 1960

GALLERY 102. Hall of Air Transportation

*Evolution of air transport of people, mail, and cargo*

**DOUGLAS DC-3.** A design milestone and perhaps the

Chuck Yeager was the first to fly faster than the speed of sound, in the **Bell X-1 *Glamorous Glennis***, named after his wife.

Below: Nicknamed *Goose*, the Grumman G-21 was designed as a commuter airplane for the wealthy but found widespread use as a commercial airliner. The amphibious airplane has floats beneath its wings, a deep fuselage that served as a hull for alighting on water, and a comfortable cabin that could accommodate four to six passengers.

single most important aircraft in air transportation history, 1935. At 16,875 pounds, the heaviest airplane hanging from the museum's ceiling

**FORD 5-AT TRI-MOTOR.** Offered dependable, safe, and relatively comfortable service when introduced in 1928

**DOUGLAS M-2.** Operated on the first airmail route between Los Angeles and Salt Lake City, 1926

**PITCAIRN PA-5 MAILWING.** Efficient, reliable airmail carrier, first flown in 1927

**NORTHROP ALPHA.** All-metal, cantilever-wing monoplane with an enclosed passenger cabin, 1930

**FAIRCHILD FC-2.** First service aircraft of Pan-American-Grace Airways (Panagra), 1928

**BOEING 247D.** First modern airliner, 1934

**DOUGLAS DC-7** (nose only). Visitors can walk through the cockpit of this 1953 airliner.

**GRUMMAN G-21** *GOOSE*. Versatile amphibian for executives and small airlines, 1937

## GALLERY 103

*This gallery contains two-person simulators that are based on a wide selection of aircraft types and are capable of 360 degrees of motion in the loop and roll modes. The occupant can take the controls of the simulator or follow a pre-planned program. Admission fee.*

## GALLERY 104. Special Exhibits

*Changing exhibits of aircraft*

## GALLERY 105. Golden Age of Flight

*Aviation between the two world wars*

**BEECH MODEL 17 STAGGERWING**. Popular general aviation aircraft of the 1930s; the museum's Staggerwing dates from 1936

Above: The most success-ful airliner in history, the Douglas DC-3 dominated both commercial and military air transportation from its introduction in 1935 until after World War II. It was the first airplane that could make money by carrying only passengers. This one flew nearly 57,000 hours for Eastern Air Lines from 1937 to 1952.

**WITTMAN CHIEF OSHKOSH *BUSTER*.** From 1931 until its retirement in 1954, this midget air racer set records, including two wins in the Goodyear Trophy races.

**CURTISS ROBIN J-1 DELUXE *OLE MISS*.** Set endurance record of 27 days over Meridian, Mississippi, 1935

**NORTHROP GAMMA 2B *POLAR STAR*.** First flight across Antarctica, 1935

**HUGHES H-1.** Aircraft in which Howard Hughes set several speed records in the 1930s

## GALLERY 106. Jet Aviation

*The development and present state of jet aviation and its related technology*

**MURAL BY KEITH FERRIS.** A large-scale depiction of important jet aircraft, 1981

**LOCKHEED XP-80 SHOOTING STAR *LULU BELL*.** First operational U.S. jet fighter, 1944

**MESSERSCHMITT ME 262 SCHWALBE (SWALLOW).** World's first operational jet fighter, 1944

**MCDONNELL FH-1 PHANTOM I.** First U.S. jet to take off and land on an aircraft carrier, 1947

**WHITTLE W.1.X.** Experimental aircraft engine that powered the British Gloster E.28/39 for taxiing trials in April 1941. Unofficially the first British turbojet to be airborne

**HEINKEL HES 3B TURBOJET.** This type of engine powered the Heinkel He 178 on the world's first flight of a turbojet-powered aircraft, 1939

**PRATT & WHITNEY JT9D.** Turbofan engine used in wide-body jet airliners

**WILLIAMS WR19.** World's smallest turbofan engine

## GALLERY 107. Early Flight

*The early history of flight*

**LILIENTHAL STANDARD GLIDER.** A glider built in 1894 by Otto Lilienthal, an experimenter who inspired Wilbur and Orville Wright

**1909 WRIGHT MILITARY FLYER.** World's first military aircraft

The Messerschmitt Me 262A-1a, the world's first operational jet fighter, outperformed the best Allied fighters of World War II but entered combat too late to have much impact on the war. This rare example was one of many German aircraft captured and returned to the United States for testing. It scored 42 victories over Russian aircraft and seven over American.

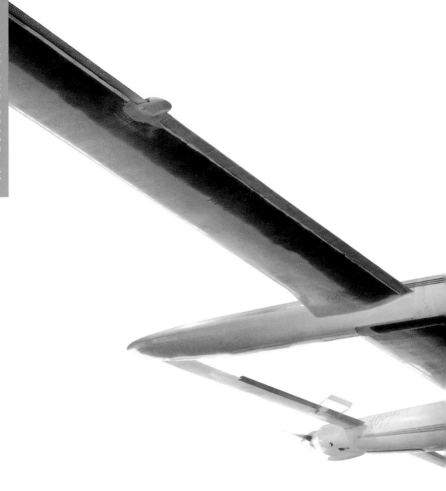

**CURTISS D-III HEADLESS PUSHER**. A favorite with U.S. exhibition pilots in 1911–12

**ECKER FLYING BOAT**. Earliest existing flying boat

**BLÉRIOT XI**. Louis Blériot made the first heavier-than-air flight across the English Channel in a similar aircraft on July 25, 1909.

**LANGLEY QUARTER-SCALE AERODROME**. One of several powered, unpiloted aircraft built and flown by Samuel P. Langley. This one made two successful flights, in 1901 and 1903

**LANGLEY AERODROME #5**. First successful flight of a powered, unpiloted heavier-than-air craft of substantial size, 1896

**AERONAUTICAL ENGINES**. Some of the in-line, radial, and rotary engines that propelled airplanes from 1907 to 1914

GALLERY 108. Independence Avenue Lobby

*The Rutan* Voyager, *flanked by two murals*

**THE RUTAN *VOYAGER*.** First aircraft to fly around the world nonstop without refueling, 1986

***THE SPACE MURAL: A COSMIC VIEW*.** Robert T. McCall's conception of the creation of the Universe, the triumph of lunar exploration, and an optimistic look at the future

***EARTH FLIGHT ENVIRONMENT*.** Eric Sloane's dramatic depiction of the remarkable ocean of air that is our atmosphere

***CONTINUUM*.** Bronze sculpture, by Charles O. Perry, outside lobby entrance, 1976

The Rutan *Voyager*, the first aircraft to fly non-stop around the world without refueling, is displayed in the south lobby.

The Lockheed U-2C, an important aerial mapping and surveillance craft since the 1950s, is a focal point of the Looking at Earth gallery.

GALLERY 109. How Things Fly

*Hands-on exhibits and demonstrations of the scientific principles that allow aircraft and spacecraft to fly*

**INTERACTIVE EXHIBITS**. Dozens of hands-on mechanical exhibits demonstrating the four forces of flight: weight, lift, thrust, and drag

**CESSNA 150**. Visitors can climb into the cockpit and manipulate the controls

**SCIENCE DEMONSTRATIONS**. Daily schedule is posted at gallery entrance

**RESOURCE CENTER**. Take-home activity sheets, teacher materials, and gallery guides

**EXPLAINERS**. High school and college students answer visitors' questions and provide information about the gallery.

GALLERY 110. Looking at Earth

*Development of technology for viewing Earth from balloons, aircraft, and spacecraft*

**DE HAVILLAND DH-4**. A British-designed and American-built World War I military aircraft later used for airmail, mapping, and photography

**LOCKHEED U-2C**. The key U.S. reconnaissance aircraft of the Cold War era, with a flight suit worn by Francis Gary Powers and memorabilia from his imprisonment in the Soviet Union; and a surveillance camera dating from the late 1950s

**EARTH OBSERVATION SATELLITES**. Prototype of TIROS, the world's first weather satellite, 1960; engineering test model of an ITOS weather satellite, 1970s; half-scale model of a GOES geostationary satellite, 1975 to the present; and models of other satellites

**LANDSAT IMAGE OF THE CHESAPEAKE BAY AREA**. A 14-foot photomural, including Washington, D.C., and Baltimore, Maryland

**WHAT'S NEW**. Developments in the science and technology of looking at Earth

GALLERY 111. Explore the Universe
*How new astronomical tools—from Galileo's telescope in the early 1600s to the latest high-tech observatories on Earth and in space—revolutionize our view of the Universe*

**EARLY ASTRONOMICAL TOOLS**. Astrolabes, quadrants, and a celestial globe dating from 1090 to the 1600s, together with replicas of other instruments

**20-FOOT TELESCOPE**. The tube and mirror from the famous telescope used by William Herschel beginning in the 1700s to study the structure and nature of the Universe

**OBSERVING CAGE AND CAMERA FROM THE 100-INCH TELESCOPE AT MT. WILSON OBSERVATORY IN SOUTHERN CALIFORNIA**. Used by astronomer Edwin Hubble, whose discoveries changed our understanding of the

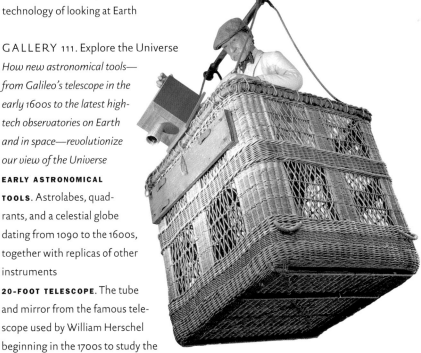

This type of basket, held aloft by a hot-air balloon, was used in early aerial photography.

## AT A GLANCE

The 1903 Wright Flyer, Charles Lindbergh's *Spirit of St. Louis*, John Glenn's *Friendship 7*, the Apollo 11 command module *Columbia,* and the walk-through Skylab orbital workshop are just a few of the attractions in this vast and exciting museum. Not to be missed are special IMAX® films on air-and-space–related topics, projected on a screen five stories high and seven stories wide, providing a breathtaking cinematic experience.

**Above: In 1927, Charles Lindbergh made the first nonstop solo transatlantic flight in the *Spirit of St. Louis*. Opposite: Lunar Module 2 is one of two remaining lunar landers built for the early Apollo missions.**

nature and motion of galaxies in the early 20th century **PRIME FOCUS SPECTROGRAPH FROM THE 200-INCH TELESCOPE AT PALOMAR OBSERVATORY IN SOUTHERN CALIFORNIA.** The most sensitive camera in the world mounted on the most powerful telescope in the world, this instrument helped astronomers in the latter half of the 20th century study the most-distant galaxies yet seen.

**HUBBLE SPACE TELESCOPE BACKUP MIRROR.** This artifact, showing the honeycomb structure that supports the mirror surface, is nearly identical to the one currently in use on the Hubble.

**CCDS AND OTHER LIGHT DETECTORS.** Digital detectors from a variety of significant ground-, air-, and space-based instruments that were designed to explore every facet of the Universe

**COBE, HUBBLE, AND CHANDRA.** Models (1/5 scale) of three spacecraft that have helped astronomers shape our current ideas on the origins and development of the Universe

## GALLERY 112. Lunar Exploration Vehicles
*Exploring the Moon*

**LUNAR MODULE.** Backup of the Apollo spacecraft that carried astronauts to the surface of the Moon in the late 1960s and early 1970s; Apollo space suit replicas

**SURVEYOR LUNAR PROBE.** Soft-landed on the Moon to study lunar soil composition and physical properties of the lunar surface, 1966–68

**LUNAR ORBITER.** Circled the Moon and mapped the entire lunar surface, 1966–67

**RANGER LUNAR PROBE.** Provided the first close-up photographs of the lunar surface, 1962–65

## GALLERY 113. Rocketry and Space Flight
*Science, technology, and the human desire to leave Earth and fly into space, from the 13th century to the present*

**EARTH TODAY.** Displays global-scale Earth science data, collected daily in near real-time. Provides visitors

with highly visual, up-to-date information about Earth's atmosphere, hydrosphere, geosphere, and biosphere

**HISTORICAL ARTIFACTS AND MODELS**. Represents some of the major contributions in the development of vehicles capable of space flight

**ROCKET ENGINES**. Propulsive devices (solid and liquid propellant) that power space boosters and maneuver spacecraft

**SPACE SUITS**. From high-altitude aviators' pressure suits to fully independent life-support space suits used on the Moon

The Space Race gallery compares U.S. and Soviet technology developed for manned lunar missions. At the left is a model of the U.S. Saturn V rocket and an Apollo space suit worn on the Moon. At the right is a model of the Soviet N-1 rocket, which failed in test flights, and a Soviet Moon suit designed for a lunar landing mission that never occurred.

## GALLERY 114. SPACE RACE

*Tells the story of the United States' and the former Soviet Union's competition in space and the race to the Moon*

**V-2**. First operational long-range ballistic missile (German), 1944–45

**AEROBEE**. Major carrier of scientific instruments for probing the upper atmosphere, 1947–85

**VIKING**. U.S. Navy sounding rocket developed for scientific purposes, 1949–55

**JUPITER-C AND VANGUARD BOOSTERS**. First two U.S. satellite launch vehicles, 1958

**SCOUT-D**. Solid-propellant launch vehicle for scientific satellites, 1961–94

**MINUTEMAN III**. U.S. Air Force intercontinental ballistic missile, 1970 to the present

**IVAN IVANOVICH, TEST FLIGHT MANNEQUIN**. Mannequin sent into space by the Soviet space program a few weeks before the first human flight, March 1961

**YURI GAGARIN FLIGHT SUIT**. Flight suit worn during training by cosmonaut Gagarin, first person in space, April 12, 1961

**JOHN GLENN SPACE SUIT**. Worn by astronaut Glenn, the first American to orbit Earth, February 1962

**SPACESUIT AND AIRLOCK FROM FIRST SPACEWALK**. Cosmonaut Alexsei Leonov became the first human to "walk" in space, March 1965

**APOLLO-SOYUZ TEST PROJECT**. First international manned space mission, 1975

**APOLLO 15 LUNAR SUIT**. Astronaut David Scott wore this suit on the Moon

**CORONA CAMERA**. The United States designed this and similar cameras to observe the Soviet Union from space

**SKYLAB ORBITAL WORKSHOP**. A walk-through, backup Skylab spacecraft, the first U.S. space station, 1973–74

**APOLLO-SOYUZ TEST PROJECT**. First international manned space mission, 1975

Skylab, America's first space station, was launched into orbit in May 1973. This large cylinder with attached solar panels is the backup Skylab orbital workshop.

The German Arado 234 from 1944, a twin-engined jet aircraft, was the world's first operational jet bomber.

**SPACE SHUTTLE**. Model of the shuttle orbiter *Columbia* on its launchpad; shuttle flight clothing and Spacelab model, 1981 to the present

**HUBBLE SPACE TELESCOPE**. Full-size test model of observatory put in orbit by Space Shuttle, 1990

GALLERY 115. Langley IMAX® Theater
*Large-format films on air-and-space–related topics are shown on a screen five stories high and seven stories wide. Admission fee. Schedule available at information desk.*

GALLERY 201. Albert Einstein Planetarium
*Lectures on the night sky and multimedia programs on astronomy and space are presented in the domed theater. The planetarium projector simulates the nighttime sky and the motions of the Sun, Moon, and planets. Admission fee.*

GALLERY 203. Sea-Air Operations
*Aircraft carrier operations from 1911 to the present*
**CARRIER HANGAR DECK**. Major aircraft from different periods in sea-air history

**BOEING F4B-4**. Biplane built for the U.S. Navy and Marine Corps, flown by Museum Director John R. Dailey's father in the 1930s

**DOUGLAS SBD DAUNTLESS**. Type of carrier-based dive bomber used during most of World War II

**GRUMMAN FM-1 WILDCAT**. Basic U.S. Navy and Marine Corps fighter aircraft at the start of World War II

**DOUGLAS A-4C SKYHAWK**. First-line naval attack aircraft of the 1950s and 1960s

**CARRIER WAR IN THE PACIFIC**. Depicts the six major aircraft-carrier battles in the Pacific during World War II

   **MODERN CARRIER AVIATION**. Developments in carrier construction, operations, roles, and missions in the nuclear age

GALLERY 205. World War II Aviation

*Fighter aircraft and related material from five countries*

**NORTH AMERICAN P-51D MUSTANG**. An outstanding fighter airplane, used in every theater of the war

**MITSUBISHI A6M5 ZERO FIGHTER**. With excellent maneuverability and range, used throughout the war by the Japanese navy

The Langley IMAX® Theater presents a variety of 70mm, large-format films. Stadium-style seating provides unobstructed views of the huge screen, which measures about 50 feet tall and 75 feet wide. The movie *To Fly* lets you experience a balloon ascension in the 1800s, roar over the Arizona landscape with the U.S. Navy's Blue Angels, soar with a hang glider off the coast of Hawaii, and blast into space with a Saturn Rocket.

The Grumman FM-1 Wild-cat was the Navy's main carrier fighter for the first two years of World War II. This version has a mechanism that allows the wings to fold back against the fuselage.

**MARTIN B-26 *FLAK BAIT* (NOSE SECTION).** Flew more missions than any other U.S. bomber in Europe

**SUPERMARINE SPITFIRE MARK VII.** A later version of the legendary British fighter that helped defeat the Germans in the Battle of Britain

**MESSERSCHMITT BF 109 *GUSTAV*.** Principal Luftwaffe fighter and the major opponent of Spitfires, Mustangs, and U.S. bombers

**MACCHI C.202 FOLGORE.** Most successful Italian fighter to see extensive service in the African campaign and in Italy and the Soviet Union

**U.S.S. *ENTERPRISE*.** Model of the carrier, constructed by Stephen Henniger

**MURAL.** *Fortresses under Fire,* by Keith Ferris, 1976

GALLERY 206. Legend, Memory, and the Great War in the Air
*The emergence of air power in World War I*
**PFALZ D.XII.** German fighter aircraft used in Hollywood films about aviation in World War I

**VOISIN VIII**. Early type of night bomber, 1915

**SPAD XIII *SMITH IV***. French fighter aircraft flown by U.S. ace Ray Brooks of the 22nd Aero Pursuit Squadron

**FOKKER D.VII**. Considered the best German fighter aircraft of World War I

**ALBATROS D.VA**. German fighter aircraft that flew on all fronts during World War I

**SOPWITH SNIPE**. British aircraft considered to be one of the best all-around single-seat fighters, although it became operational only late in the war

**GERMAN FACTORY SCENE**. World War I mass-production techniques, with original equipment

**HOLLYWOOD FILMS PORTRAYING A ROMANTIC IMAGE OF THE "KNIGHTS OF THE AIR."**

GALLERY 207. Exploring the Planets
*History and achievements of planetary exploration, both Earth-based and by spacecraft*

***VOYAGER***. Full-scale replica of the spacecraft that explored Jupiter, Saturn, Uranus, and Neptune in the 1970s and 1980s

**THE *VIKING* VIEW OF MARS**. Backup spacecraft equipment for the *Viking* landers; video, *Mars: The Movie*

**A PIECE OF MARS?**. Meteorite collected in Antarctica that may have come from Mars

The North American P-51D Mustang escorted high-altitude Allied bombers deep into Europe.

Britain developed the Sopwith Snipe late in World War I to replace its Sopwith Camel. Pictured here is a Sopwith 7F.1 Snipe, the only survivor of its type.

**SURVEYOR 3 TELEVISION CAMERA**. Retrieved from the surface of the Moon by the Apollo 12 astronauts **"WHAT'S NEW."** Current planetary exploration

GALLERY 208. Pioneers of Flight
*Famous "firsts" and record setters*
**LOCKHEED SIRIUS *TINGMISSARTOQ***. Flown by Charles and Anne Lindbergh on airline route–mapping flights, 1930s
**LOCKHEED 5B VEGA**. First solo flight across the Atlantic, by Amelia Earhart, 1932
**FOKKER T-2**. First nonstop U.S. transcontinental flight, 1923
**BELL 206L-1 LONGRANGER II *SPIRIT OF TEXAS***. First helicopter to travel around the world, piloted by H. Ross Perot Jr. and J. Coburn, 1982
**EXTRA 260**. National Aerobatic championship aircraft flown by Patty Wagstaff, 1991

**HAWTHORNE C. GREY BALLOON BASKET AND EQUIPMENT**. Ushered in the era of stratospheric balloon flights, 1927

***GOSSAMER CONDOR***. First successful human-powered aircraft, 1977

**DOUGLAS WORLD CRUISER *CHICAGO***. First around-the-world flight, 1924

***EXPLORER II* GONDOLA**. This cabin and its balloon rose to a height never before achieved and made valuable scientific observations, 1935

**BLACK WINGS: THE AMERICAN BLACK IN AVIATION**. Exhibit chronicles the struggle of African Americans to earn a place in aeronautics and space flight in the United States

GALLERY 209. The Wright Brothers & the Invention of the Aerial Age (opening April 2003)
*This exhibition marks the centennial of flight with an in-depth examination of the Wright brothers' invention of the airplane and its initial impact on society. The 1903 Wright Flyer is displayed at eye level, offering visitors an opportunity to see this world-changing invention up close and in detail.*

**1903 WRIGHT FLYER**. Original airplane flown at Kitty Hawk, North Carolina, on December 17, 1903

**1900 WRIGHT GLIDER (REPRODUCTION)**. First aircraft with which the Wrights made piloted gliding flights

**WRIGHT BICYCLE**. One of only five original Wright brothers' bicycles known to exist

**WRIGHT WIND TUNNEL (REPRODUCTION)**. Instrument the Wright brothers used to gather the aerodynamic data from which they built their aircraft

**In 1932, Amelia Earhart flew this Lockheed 5B Vega solo across the Atlantic and nonstop across the United States.**

Go Baby

**MEMORABILIA**. Mementos and souvenirs from the Wrights' historic demonstration flights in Europe and America in 1908 and 1909

**HISTORIC MOTION PICTURES**. Rare historic film footage of the Wright brothers' flights

**RARE ARTWORK**. Examples of contemporary paintings and other artwork capturing the beginning of the aviation age

**Top: Five huge F-1 rocket engines were needed to lift the 30-story-tall Saturn V rocket. Bottom: Using a rover like this one, Apollo 17 astronauts spent a record 22 hours exploring the lunar surface and collecting rock and soil samples.**

GALLERY 210. Apollo to the Moon
*Triumph of manned space flight in the 1960s and early 1970s, from Project Mercury through the Apollo Moon landings*

**F-1 ENGINE**. Full-size, with cutaway of first-stage rocket engine used on the Saturn V rocket

**SPACE TOOLS AND EQUIPMENT**. Used during the Apollo missions

**LUNAR SCENES**. Showing the Lunar Rover and astronauts at work on the Moon

**SATURN BOOSTERS**. Models of Saturn IB and Saturn V rockets

**LUNAR SAMPLES**. Four types of lunar soil and rocks

**SPACE FOOD**. How astronauts' and cosmonauts' food has changed

**SPACE SUITS**. Worn on the Moon by Apollo astronauts Eugene Cernan, Neil Armstrong, and Edwin "Buzz" Aldrin

GALLERY 211. Flight and the Arts
*Selections from the permanent art collection*

GALLERY 213. Beyond the Limits: Flight Enters the Computer Age
*How computers are used in aerospace design and operations*

**X-29 (FULL-SCALE MODEL)**. Forward-swept-wing airplane

**CRAY-1 SUPERCOMPUTER**. Once the world's fastest computer

**INTERACTIVE COMPUTERS**. Visitors can try out computer-aided design, flight simulation, airline scheduling, and flight testing.

*Mural Master Study: Horizontal* **by Robert T. McCall, 1975, acrylic on canvas, 58 x 229 cm (23 x 90 in.).**

**SPACE STATION THEATER**. Films on flight simulation, the X-29, and computer software

**HIMAT**. Robot airplane that pioneered the use of fly-by-wire technology, in which a computer, not the pilot, controls the aircraft

**MINUTEMAN III ICBM GUIDANCE AND CONTROL SYSTEM.** The brain of the Minuteman missile, the standard U.S. land-based intercontinental ballistic missile

**MOTOROLA IRIDIUM SATELLITE.** Flight backup craft for the world's first global, satellite-based telephone network, 1998

**GLOBAL POSITIONING SATELLITE (1/4-SCALE MODEL).** Space-based constellation of satellites used for precise navigation and position location

## PAUL E. GARBER PRESERVATION, RESTORATION AND STORAGE FACILITY

The Paul E. Garber Preservation, Restoration and Storage Facility in Suitland, Maryland, houses the National Air and Space Museum's reserve collection of historically significant aircraft, spacecraft, and other artifacts.

Used since the mid-1950s as a storage and restoration center, the facility now has several buildings open to the public as a "no frills" museum. Exhibited here are more than 150 aircraft, as well as many spacecraft, engines, propellers, and other flight-related objects. Guided tours include a behind-the-scenes look at the workshop where all phases of the restoration process are handled—from upholstery repair to engine reconstruction.

The facility is named for the late Paul E. Garber, historian emeritus and Ramsey Fellow of the National Air and Space Museum, who joined the Smithsonian Institution in 1920 and was responsible for acquiring a large portion of the aeronautical collection.

Above: A restoration volunteer at the Garber Facility explains aspects of restoring the Pitts Special S-1C *Little Stinker*. Below: Max Gainer, restoration volunteer, and Rich Horigan, restoration specialist, work on the wings of the Nieuport 28C.1.

**LOCKHEED P-38J LIGHTNING, HAWKER HURRICANE, AND FOCKE-WULF FW 190.** Just a few of the famous World War II fighter planes on display

**ROSCOE TURNER'S RT-14 *METEOR*.** A racer from the golden age of aviation

**CURTISS JN-4D JENNY.** An aircraft made famous by the barnstormers after World War I

**NORTH AMERICAN F-86A AND MIG-15.** Arch rivals in the Korean War

## STEVEN F. UDVAR-HAZY CENTER

A companion facility to the National Air and Space Museum that will open in 2003, the Steven F. Udvar-Hazy Center will eventually display nearly 200 aircraft, more than 100 spacecraft, and thousands of other artifacts related to the history of flight, many of which have never before been exhibited.

The center, at Washington Dulles International Airport, will be enormous—the aviation hangar alone

The Steven F. Udvar-Hazy Center is being built at Washington Dulles International Airport in northern Virginia. In addition to nearly 200 airplanes and more than 100 spacecraft, its 760,000 square feet will include space for exhibit hangars, a restoration shop, collections storage, classrooms, archives, a large-format theater, restaurants, and museum stores.

**On display in the lower level of the National Air and Space Museum's store are a few artifacts from the museum's collection, including a Pitts Special aerobatic biplane.**

will be more than three football fields long and ten stories tall, large enough to contain the entire National Air and Space building on the National Mall. It will house the SR-71 Blackbird, the prototype Space Shuttle orbiter *Enterprise,* the fully restored B-29 Superfortress *Enola Gay,* the Boeing B-17D *Swoose,* and the Boeing 367-80 protoype of the 707 airliner, together with hundreds of other aircraft, spacecraft, rockets, engines, and more.

The museum's restoration facility will be located at the Udvar-Hazy Center and will be almost twice the size of the current workshop at the Garber Facility. The center also will have an observation tower from which to watch aircraft taking off and landing at the adjacent runways. A large-format theater and an educational resource center will be part of the facility as well.

## TOURS OF THE GARBER FACILITY

Free public tours of the Garber Facility are available Monday through Friday at 10 A.M. and Saturday and Sunday at 10 A.M. and 1 P.M. Reservations must be made at least two weeks in advance. Call 202-357-1400 or 202-357-1505 (TTY) between 9 A.M. and 3:15 P.M., Monday through Friday, or write to: Office of Tours and Reservations, Room 1153A, National Air and Space Museum, Washington, D.C. 20560-0308.

Individuals or groups of up to 40 may take the guided tours, which last about three hours. Special tours for disabled visitors are available on request. Note: There is no heating or air-conditioning in the warehouse-type exhibit areas.

The Garber Facility will be closed for tours when the museum begins moving artifacts to the Udvar-Hazy Center at Washington Dulles International Airport. Please call the Office of Tours and Reservations or visit www.nasm.si.edu for the current status of tours.

In the Independence Avenue lobby

## TOURS OF THE NATIONAL AIR AND SPACE MUSEUM

Free public tours are offered daily at 10:15 A.M. and 1 P.M.; no advance reservations are needed. Tours for school groups (25 to 125 people) and other organizations must be scheduled at least three weeks in advance. Call 202-357-1400, or 202-357-1505 (TTY).

## FREE SCIENCE DEMONSTRATIONS

A daily schedule is posted at the entrance to gallery 109.

## FILMS AND PLANETARIUM SHOWS

Films on air-and-space–related topics are projected on a huge screen in the Langley IMAX® Theater, with continuous showings daily. The Albert Einstein Planetarium also has presentations daily. Tickets can be purchased up to two weeks in advance. Check the museum's Web site or call 202-357-1686 for schedules.

## EDUCATIONAL SERVICES

Information on daily events for children and families is available at the information desk or by calling 202-786-2106. The museum offers workshops, orientations, materials for educators, and visitors guides. Ask for a program brochure and other information at the information desk.

## WHERE TO EAT

Food service is available on the first floor at the east end of the museum.

## MUSEUM STORES

Near the Mall entrance and on the second floor. Items for sale include books, postcards, slides, posters, models, souvenirs, T-shirts, and first-day stamp covers.

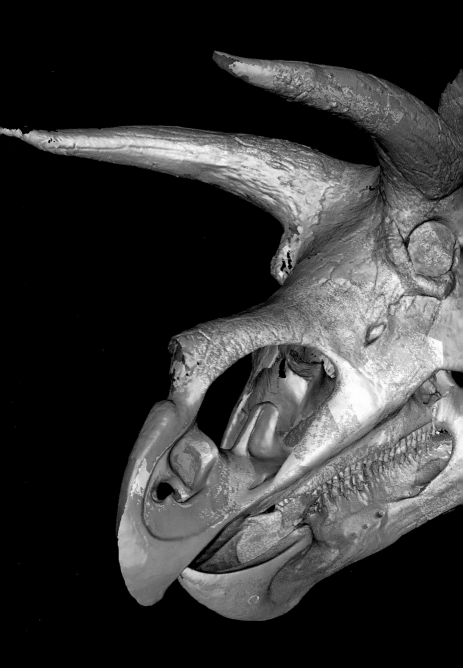

The first "digital dinosaur" is on permanent display in the Dinosaur Hall. Three-dimensional modeling based on surface scans such as this one made possible the world's most accurate reconstruction of one of the most popular dinosaurs, the *Triceratops*. Opposite top: Stunning in their architectural shells, snails like this one highlight the biological collections.

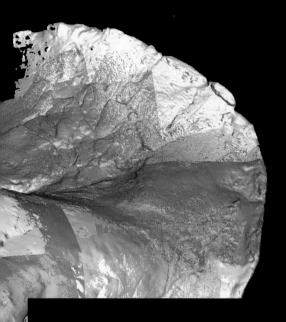

# NATIONAL MUSEUM OF NATURAL HISTORY

Constitution Avenue (accessible entrance) at 10th Street, NW. Mall entrance: Madison Drive between 9th and 12th Streets, NW. Open daily, except December 25, 10 A.M. to 5:30 P.M.; Samuel C. Johnson Theater and Atrium Café, featuring live jazz beginning at 5:30 P.M., open Friday until 10 P.M. Metrorail: Federal Triangle station. Smithsonian information: 202-357-2700 TTY: 202-357-1729. www.mnh.si.edu

The National Museum of Natural History is dedicated to understanding the natural world and our place in it. As the nation's largest research museum, it is a treasure house of more than 121 million specimens of plants, animals, rocks, gems and minerals, fossils, and human cultural artifacts. This encyclopedic collection is an essential resource for scientists studying the earth sciences, the biological world, and human origins and cultures. Exhibitions and - educational programs attract large numbers of visitors every year to the museum's green-domed Beaux-Arts building, one of Washington's best-known landmarks.

Only a tiny portion of the collection is on public display. Many of the objects are housed in the Smithsonian's Museum Support Center in Suitland, Maryland, which provides state-of-the-art conditions

Researchers stand in one of the many corridors in the Bird Collection storage area, which holds a total of 450,000 bird skins.

for the storage and conservation of research collections. Behind the scenes in the laboratories and offices at the museum and the support center, more than 100 scholars conduct research in association with colleagues from universities, other museums, and government agencies.

The story told in these halls is the story of our planet from its wild, fiery beginnings to its transformation over 4.6 billion years by a marvelous web of evolving life, including our own species. Living and nonliving, art and artifact: taken together, they reveal a wondrous and complex world.

## GROUND FLOOR

Just inside the Constitution Avenue entrance is an exhibit that introduces the wonders of the museum. Among the 250 objects highlighted are amethysts and pyrite crystals, a 700,000-year-old hand ax from Kenya, pottery by the renowned Pueblo artists Maria Martinez and Nampeo, totem poles from the Northwest Coast, a gigantic tooth from a fossil shark, meteorites, a calcite-encrusted bird's nest, and morpho butterflies from South America.

Beyond the lobby, by the museum store, stands a huge stone disc used as money on Yap in the Caroline Islands and the entrance to the Discovery Center housing the Atrium Café and the glass elevator to the Samuel C. Johnson Theater showing 2-D and 3-D IMAX® films.

**Above: The museum holds collections of great diversity and beauty, typified by these morpho butterflies. Below: A film still from *Galapagos* captures the drama of this 3-D IMAX® film.**

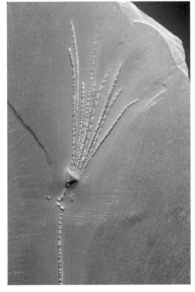

Top: Ammonites, relatives of the modern pearly nautilus, were some of the most abundant and diverse invertebrates during the Mesozoic. Bottom: Crinoids, animals that are sometimes called sea lilies, populated the Paleozoic seas.

Baird Auditorium, used for lectures, concerts, films, and other special events, is also located on the ground floor. Outside the auditorium is Baird Gallery, where almost 300 mounted species of birds of the eastern United States are on display. They include some superb examples of hawks and eagles.

## FIRST FLOOR

### THE ROTUNDA

The largest mounted elephant in the world, the Fenykovi elephant, holds sway over the Rotunda of the museum. The African bull elephant, standing 13'2" high at the shoulder and weighing in at nearly 12 tons, is incorporated into a diorama depicting the natural ecological habitat of an African elephant living in Angola. The plants and animals in the diorama are a combination of actual specimens, models, and casts from the museum's vast scientific collections. A panoramic video display of the African savanna and its inhabitants brings the elephant diorama alive. A surrounding soundscape broadcasts the trumpet sounds of elephants, birdcalls, insects buzzing and snakes hissing, alerting visitors that this is a museum about nature.

In the Rotunda's surrounding ambulatory on the second floor, interpretive exhibits look more closely at the elephant's anatomy, evolution, and impact on African cultures. An audio-described tour of the Rotunda's architecture highlights the unique features of this grand, four-story room. An interactive kiosk on the first floor takes the visitors "Inside Natural History" to learn about the research activities of the scientific departments of the museum.

The eight-sided Rotunda is one of Washington, D.C.'s splendid spaces. It is 125 feet high from the mar-

ble floor to the tiled dome. The first-story columns are Doric in style, and the second- and third-story columns are Roman and Ionic. Many of the architectural details are best seen from the second-floor Rotunda balcony.

## FOSSILS: THE HISTORY OF LIFE

This major exhibition presents highlights from the beginnings of life in the sea 3.5 billion years ago.

**EARLIEST TRACES OF LIFE** includes the oldest fossil, a cabbage-size 3.5-billion-year-old mass built by microorganisms. An animated film and a dramatic mural trace the origin and evolution of life, while a time column standing more than 27 feet high shows an index of geologic time.

**The museum's African bull elephant welcomes visitors to the majestic four-story Rotunda. The diorama depicts his natural ecological habitat in Angola.**

**A GRAND OPENING: FOSSILS GALORE** documents the dramatic explosion of hard-shelled life at the beginning of the Paleozoic Era 570 million years ago. Rare 530-million-year-old fossilized soft-bodied animals of the Burgess Shale are on display here. These fossils, which are among the Smithsonian's greatest finds, were discovered in 1910 by the Institution's fourth Secretary, geologist Charles D. Walcott.

**LIFE IN THE ANCIENT SEAS** showcases prehistoric marine life, emphasizing evolutionary innovations and describing the existence of these unfamiliar animals and plants. Through sound and lighting, the hall gives the visitor the feeling of being underwater in the marine realm. Among the approximately 2,000 fossils on exhibit are the 45-foot-long skeleton of *Basilosaurus* (an early whale) and a spectacular slab of sea lilies from the early Carboniferous period 345 to 325 million years ago. To bring these creatures to life, the exhibition features a series of murals showing the fleshed-out animals these fossils once were and a full-scale diorama of a 250-million-year-old reef made of more than 100,000 models.

**THE CONQUEST OF LAND** focuses on the earliest plants and animals to evolve the complex adaptations needed to live on land. In an animated video evoking

With dioramas and murals, exhibitions re-create part of the Paleozoic Reef (top) and the world of a mosasaur (bottom), which, like the dinosaurs, died out 65 million years ago. The lobe-finned fishes of the Late Devonian period (middle) may have "walked" to large pools of water.

television coverage of the first lunar landing, characters Frank Anchorfish and Arthur Pod explain what plants and animals needed to pioneer the harsh, dry terrestrial environment. Just beyond an arbor formed by a diorama of the first forests are still more fossils: specimens of a 16-foot fossil of an early tree, *Callixylon;* other fossil trees and smaller plants from the ancient coal forests of North America; and skeletons of many amphibians. Completing the section are displays on the seed and the amniotic egg—the two evolutionary innovations that secured the conquest of land for plants and animals.

**REPTILES: MASTERS OF LAND** features the skeletons of dinosaurs, the great reptiles that dominated Earth for 140 million years until their extinction about 65 million years ago.

*Diplodocus,* an 80-foot-long member of the sauropod family of dinosaurs, the largest land-dwelling animals of all time, towers over skeletons of *Camptosaurus, Stegosaurus,* and *Allosaurus,* a fearsome predator. The Smithsonian's *Triceratops* is the world's first digital dinosaur, a product of surface scanning and computer prototyping that corrected inaccuracies in the museum's original 1905 skeleton. This new exhibit shows *Triceratops* in a more accurate posture, facing off with *Tyrannosaurus rex.* The exhibit also showcases other relatives of *Triceratops,* including the two-horned *Diceratops* (the only known specimen), *Styracosaurus* (a full skeletal mount of a baby), *Centrosaurus, Protoceratops, Begac-*

**The 80-foot-long skeleton of *Diplodocus* dominates the Dinosaur Hall. A member of the sauropod family, it was one of the largest animals ever to have walked the earth.**

eratops, *Psittacosaurus,* and four bony-domed dinosaurs, the *Pachycephalosaurs.* Visitors can touch a cast horn core of *Triceratops* and a bronze skull of a miniature *Triceratops,* and use an interactive video, which shows the entire process of conserving, molding and casting, laser scanning, prototyping, and researching the posture of the *Triceratops.*

A cast of *Tyrannosaurus rex,* king of the tyrant reptiles, looms over visitors as they climb the steps up to the Dinosaur Hall. Visitors witness this chance meeting between *T. rex* and its Late Cretaceous counterpart, *Triceratops.*

**MAMMALS IN THE LIMELIGHT** focuses on the spectacular explosion of mammalian evolution following the extinction of dinosaurs. Four huge murals re-create

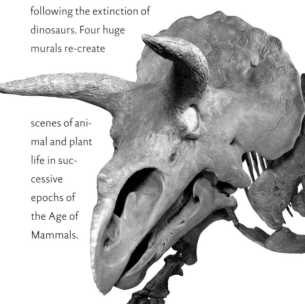

scenes of animal and plant life in successive epochs of the Age of Mammals.

The murals provide settings for fossil specimens, including mounted skeletons, many of them assembled from fossils unearthed in the American West by Smithsonian scientists. The different stages of horse evolution are shown in fossil specimens, an animated film, and a mural. To learn more about mammals and see more fossils, visit the Behring Family Hall of Mammals opening in the fall of 2003.

### FOSSILAB

FossiLab is a working paleontology laboratory where visitors can watch skilled volunteers and museum staff perform various tasks of fossil preparation and research. Exhibits surrounding the lab explain what fossils are, what activities are likely to be occurring in FossiLab, and why we study fossils.

### ICE AGE MAMMALS AND THE EMERGENCE OF MAN

The Ice Age was one of the most extraordinary periods in Earth's history. At the entrance to this exhibition, a cast of a 24,800-year-old mammoth tusk, beautifully engraved by an early artist, symbolizes the emergence of humans as a dominant influence on the environment. Mounted skeletons of some of the

The skeleton of *Hyracotherium,* an ancestral horse, marks the entrance to the fossil mammal hall, Mammals in the Limelight.

largest Ice Age mammals dominate the hall: a giant ground sloth, a woolly mammoth, and an Irish elk. Also on exhibit is an Ice Age bison, freeze-dried by nature and recovered by gold miners in Alaska. A life-size tableau of a Neanderthal burial shows that at least 70,000 years ago they carefully buried their dead and may have believed in an afterlife.

## ASIAN AND PACIFIC CULTURES

Crafts and objects from the daily life of peoples from Asia, India, and the Pacific are seen in this exhibition. Everyday objects form a central display about the various nationalities of Asia. A diorama presents a scene from a Chinese opera. A Confucian shrine and other exhibits tell about Asian music, calligraphy, and language; the music and crafts of Thailand, India, and Pakistan; and the shadow puppets of Malaysia. Objects of daily life from China and the Ryukyu Islands are shown, along with a room from a Korean house. The ancient Cambodian Khmer culture is featured, as is the imposing figure of a Fijian high chief wearing ceremonial black-and-white painted bark cloth.

In the Pacific Islands area are exhibits devoted to the Native peoples of Indonesia, Melanesia, Polynesia, Micronesia, Australia, New Zealand, and the Philip-

Above: The woolly mammoth—an extinct elephant species that once abounded in North America and northern Eurasia—reached enormous size during the Ice Age. This skeleton is on display in the Ice Age Hall.

pines. Among them is a diorama showing tattooing as practiced by the Maoris of New Zealand. Other displays feature boomerangs and bark painting by aborigines of Arnhem Land, sailing and fishing in Polynesia, and rice growing in the Philippines. One of the famous massive stone heads from Easter Island stands at the Rotunda entrance to the hall.

## AFRICAN HISTORY AND CULTURES

Rich and resonant voices from Africa and the African Diaspora—together with objects both commonplace and extraordinary—express the complexity of African lives and cultures. Africa's most striking characteristics are its immense size and wide variety of peoples. More than three times the size of the continental United States, Africa today is home to more than 300 million people inhabiting 54 countries. The African continent is divided by the boundaries of its nation-states as well as by diverse language groups, cultures, ecological zones, and histories.

"African Voices" resonates with the dynamism of

Top: In this scene from a traditional Chinese opera, advisors warn the queen mother of a plot to usurp the throne of the infant emperor of the Ming dynasty. Opposite bottom: A stone head carved of soft volcanic rock from Easter Island in the South Pacific.

contemporary African culture. It examines the overlapping, continuously broadening spheres of African influence—historical and contemporary, local and international—in the realms of family, work, commerce, and the natural environment. Objects such as a 17th-century cast brass head from the Benin Kingdom of Nigeria, a late-19th-century carved wooden staff by the Luba of Zaire, and decorative fiber headwear from 19th- and 20th-century Zaire show the aesthetic dimensions of leadership in certain African societies. A late-19th-century copper-and-brass image made by the Kota peoples of Gabon and a contemporary Afro-Cuban altar demonstrate the enduring presence of African belief systems on the African continent and in Africa's Diaspora. Akan gold weights, Ethiopian silver crosses, and decorated ceramic vessels explore the history of metallurgy and pottery in diverse regions of Africa. Objects used in everyday life, contemporary fashion, children's toys, musical instruments, and excerpts from oral poetry, song, and literary texts illustrate the transatlantic connection between Africa and the Americas.

**Top: This Brazilian sculpture from the "African Voices" exhibit in the Hall of African History and Culture is based on an ancient *dikenga* symbol of Kongo people of Central Africa. A *dikenga* represents a crossroads—spiritual, actual, or both. Bottom: This 18th-century brass head of an *oba*, or king, is from the Benin Kingdom, now a part of Nigeria. The opening on top once held a carved ivory tusk depicting the glories of the *oba*'s reign.**

### ESKIMO AND INDIAN CULTURES

This hall is arranged according to cultural areas—regions in which Native American cultures are broadly similar through shared histories and adaptations to similar environments. Near the Rotunda, a diorama depicts the adaptations of northern peoples to harsh Arctic conditions. Displays on seal hunting, ice fishing, and igloo construction lead to an exhibit of Eskimo art. Following the section on the Arctic region is the Eastern Woodland area, where a birch-bark canoe, lacrosse sticks, and other objects are displayed. Visitors can also find entrances to the lobby of the Samuel C. Johnson IMAX® Theater in this hall.

At the far end of the hall is a collection of Northwest Coast art objects, including a superb display of

masks. Exhibits on Native American culture are produced by the museum in association with Native people. Seminole Interpretations presents traditional and contemporary aspects of life among this Florida tribe today. A display of baskets made by tribal masters from all over the country is on view. In a five-minute video, Mary Adams, a master Mohawk basket maker, talks about her craft.

Other exhibits portray Native American cultures of California, the southwestern United States, Mexico, Guatemala, the Andean region, Panama, the West Indies, the South American tropical forest, Patagonia, and Tierra del Fuego.

### THE MIGHTY MARLIN

Alfred C. Glassell caught the world-record black marlin off the coast of Peru in 1953 and donated the model of this famous catch to the museum. It reaches

**Top: Carving in relief was a highly developed art by tribes of the Northwest Coast. This conventional animal design was carved on the side of a box made by a member of the Haida tribe. Bottom: A model of the world-record black marlin dominates "The Mighty Marlin" exhibition.**

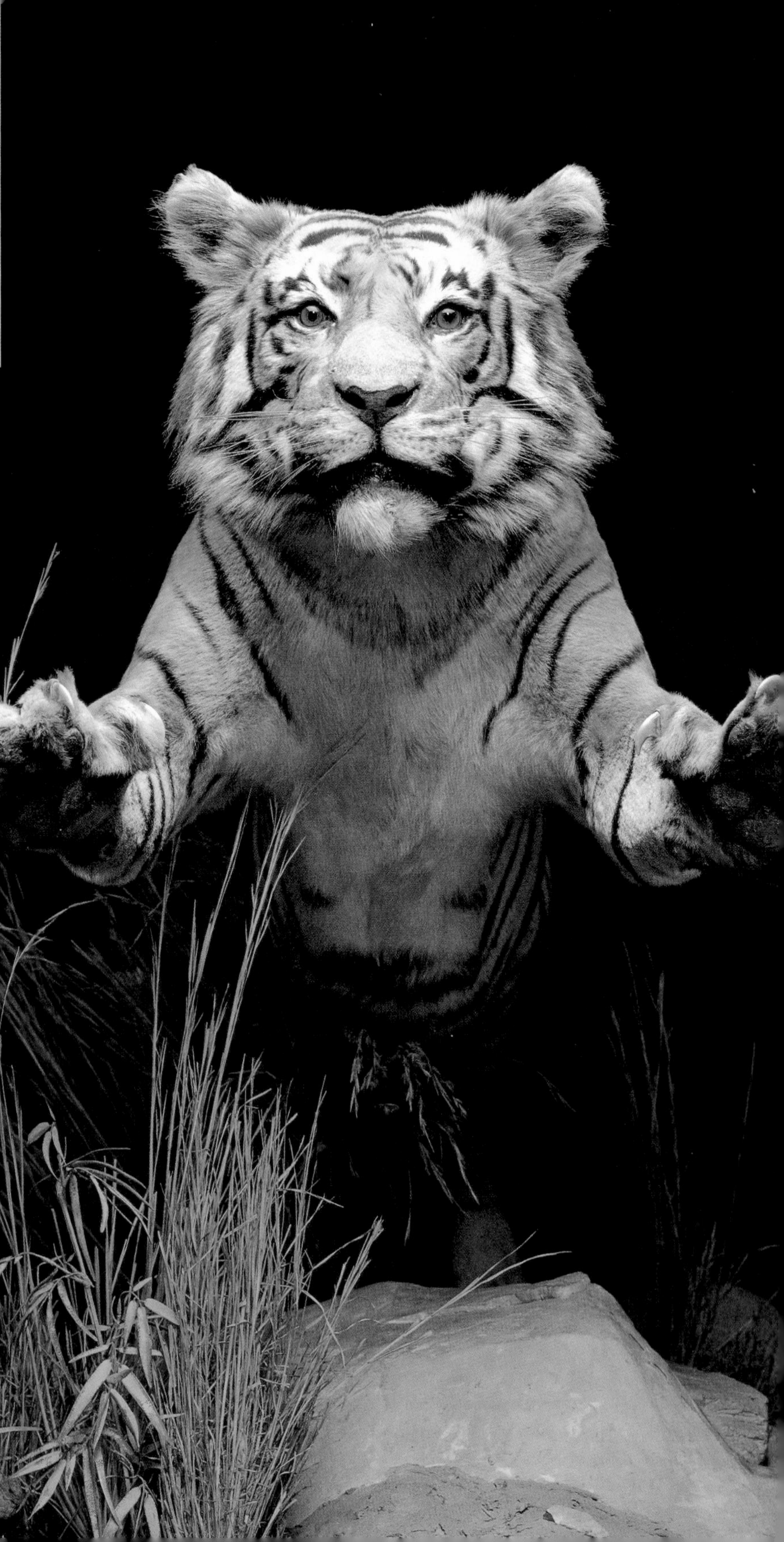

nearly 15 feet in length and weighed 1,560 pounds. Facts about the marlin and other members of the billfish family are highlighted in the exhibit. A short video focuses on the "big catch" as well as research activities of scientists in the museum's Fish Division who study fish larvae to reveal fish family secrets.

## MAMMALS

Opening in the fall of 2003, the Behring Family Hall of Mammals will demonstrate to visitors that all mammals, past and present, are related to one another by virtue of common descent. Visitors will learn that, as mammals, they belong to an ancient lineage that stretches back to before the time of dinosaurs. As living mammals, they share certain characteristics that scientists use to identify this group. All mammals have hair, nurse on milk, and have unique hearing apparatus that evolved from a jawbone—characteristics that humans share. You are a part of the great diversity of mammals. In this new hall, we invite you to join the mammal family reunion.

The Behring Family Hall of Mammals will combine a passionate and detailed commitment to scholarship with fresh interpretive approaches custom-designed to meet the needs of visitors. The exhibition will show-case the museum's collections and take full advantage of the exciting array of new learning technologies, which allow for both interactivity and in-depth content. Visit the grassland, desert, and forest of Africa: get up close to a giraffe, see how lions hunt large prey, find out about bears who lived here more than five million years ago. Wander through Australia, where ancient mammals flourished and today is the only place in the world inhabited by all three mammal groups—monotremes, marsupials, and placentals. Visit the Northern Forest of our continent and see how mammals protect themselves from the cold; then travel to the North American Prairie. Meet the prong-horn that can run faster than any mammal; discover why bison are so well suited to this environment and

In this reproduction, a Bengal tiger, the world's largest cat, lunges as if to capture a deer. Smithsonian scientists have worked with Nepalese colleagues to study and conserve the tiger, but this legendary creature's survival remains threatened.

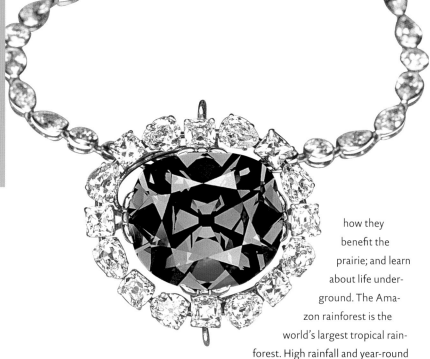

Above: The 45.5-carat Hope diamond is the best-known and largest blue diamond in the world. Below: The platinum and diamond earrings of Marie Antoinette.

how they benefit the prairie; and learn about life underground. The Amazon rainforest is the world's largest tropical rainforest. High rainfall and year-round warm temperatures support layers of evergreen plants and set the stage for crowded conditions. Come see how rainforest mammals have divided up these abundant resources from the shady forest floor to the canopy above. The Behring Family Hall of Mammals will be set within a dramatic, well-lit space restored to its impressive original architecture.

## SECOND FLOOR

### JANET ANNENBERG HOOKER HALL OF GEOLOGY, GEMS, AND MINERALS

This new hall, located off the second-floor Rotunda balcony, is the world's most comprehensive Earth science complex. The legendary Hope diamond—a must for every museum visitor—is the star attraction in the Harry Winston Gallery. The 45.5-carat blue diamond resides in a custom-made exhibit case and vault, and rotates through beams of light that makes the gem and its magnificent setting sparkle. Named for Henry Philip Hope of England, who once owned it, the diamond is still in the setting made for Evelyn Walsh McLean of Washington, D.C., the dia-

mond's last private owner. Acquired from her estate in 1949 by the New York jewelry firm of Harry Winston, Inc., the rare and magnificent gem was given to the Smithsonian by Harry Winston in 1958.

Spectacular examples of other geological objects that represent the themes of the hall are also featured in the Harry Winston Gallery: huge quartz crystals from Africa; one of the largest sheets of naturally occurring, nearly pure copper in existence; a sandstone "sculpture" created by water within the earth; polished gneiss born from heat and pressure deep within the earth; and a ring-shaped meteorite from outer space.

The National Gem Collection Gallery includes the Marie Antoinette ear-

**Above: Three impressive tourmalines are examples of specimens derived from pegmatite deposits, where large and rare crystals form. Below: The 1,371-pound "Ring" meteorite, looking like a piece of contemporary sculpture, is one of the many chunks of metal and rock that have fallen to the earth from outer space and are now in the museum's collection.**

**Specially designed airtight cases in the Moon, Meteorites, and Solar System Gallery hold several Moon rocks that help tell the story of the Moon's evolution.**

rings (one of the last gifts from King Louis XVI to his queen), the 127-carat Portuguese diamond, the Rosser Reeves ruby with its unparalleled six-rayed star, and the Hooker starburst diamonds, among the most perfect of their kind.

Other highlights of the Janet Annenberg Hooker Hall are a gallery displaying some 2,500 of the most spectacular crystals and minerals from the National Mineral Collections. A simulated mine shows how crystal pockets, ore veins, and other rocks and minerals formed within the earth. How rocks have been built, bent, broken, and baked in ages past is the subject of the Rocks Gallery. Plate tectonics is explained in a display and theater that show how the heat of Earth's interior drives the movement of the vast plates that form its outermost layer. Earthquakes and volcanoes are among the most visible results of this plate movement, and the exhibit highlights museum volcanologists' contributions to our understanding of these processes. Completing the exhibition is the Moon, Meteorites, and Solar System Gallery, featuring Moon rocks, a Mars meteorite you can touch, extensive displays of many other meteorites, and interstellar dust.

This hall shows the distinctive environments and resources of four South American regions and the different ways in which cultures have adapted to them during the prehistoric, colonial, and modern eras. A mural and diorama show the first region—the great Patagonian grasslands—as they looked in the 19th century. A hunt is in progress: nomadic Tehuelche Indians armed with bolas ride across the plains in pursuit of fleeing rhea birds. A display of the great trunks, branches, and vines of a lifelike tropical rainforest introduces the next region—the tropics. Despite its lush vegetation, this region supports only marginal

agriculture, and the tribes that live in the forest depend on wild foods. The weapons, brightly colored ornaments, and everyday tools of one of the tribes, the Waiwai, are exhibited. Along the arid Pacific coastlands, the third region, fishing and irrigation of farmland helped support large prehistoric populations. A diorama features a balsa raft of the kind coastal people used for thousands of years. The culture of the fourth region—the high Andean mountain valleys—is sustained by abundant potato and corn crops. This region is vividly portrayed in a three-dimensional re-creation

**Tehuelche Indians, nomadic hunters of the South American grasslands, pursue flightless rheas in this diorama.**

of a town plaza featuring a marketplace and church facade. Objects from the Inca civilization are exhibited beneath a mural of a mountain citadel.

### ORIGINS OF WESTERN CULTURE

This exhibit traces the increasing complexity of Western civilization from the end of the Ice Age, about 10,000 years ago, to about A.D. 500. Ice Age flint tools, such as knives and projectile points, and a reconstructed cave with paintings of animals illustrate human dependence on hunting.

After the Ice Age, people in southwestern Asia began the shift to farming as a way of life. A diorama re-creates a scene from Ali Kosh, one of the earliest farming villages. Technological advances accompanied the spread of agriculture. Egyptian pottery from 4000 B.C.E. is shown together with increasingly sophisticated stone and bone tools from Europe. Another diorama shows the Mesopotamian city of Larsa in 1801 B.C.E

The growing complexity of urban life fostered a new form of political and social organization called the state, which eventually led to the formation of empires. The complexity of ancient societies is reflected in their burial customs, illustrated in a display of the Bronze Age tombs of Bab-edh-Dhra in Jordan. *City of the Dead,* a video about Smithsonian investigations of the Bronze Age tombs, is shown in the Gilgamesh Theater.

"Frozen in Time: The Icemen" re-creates the famous Alpine ice mummy found in 1991 and shows him as he might have looked in life, some

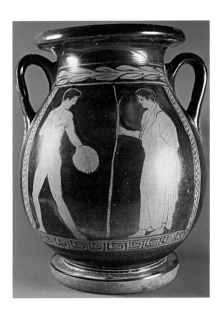

5,300 years ago. All the items of clothing and equipment shown here were reproduced for this exhibit by the same workshop that produced the exhibit for the Iceman's "home" museum, the South Tyrol Museum of Archaeology, in Bolzano, Italy, where it is currently housed and displayed. Much of the Iceman's clothing and equipment was made of perishable organic materials that normally would not have survived burial, and many of his possessions are unique and previously unknown in the archaeological record. The Iceman sports the oldest tattoos ever seen, some 57 short, black lines, usually clustered in groups. Often visible now only under infrared light, many of these marks occur on traditional acupuncture points used for treating arthritis. On display are a touchable reproduction of the copper ax, which was

**Above: Elements of classical Greek civilization are revealed in this black-and-red figure Attic vase. Left: Roman glass was a major item of trade throughout the empire and, after the invention of mass-production techniques, supplanted pottery for several everyday uses. Opposite top: A diorama re-creates one of two tombs discovered in a Bronze Age (3100 B.C.E.) cemetery complex at Bab-edh-Dhra, Jordan. Opposite bottom: This cuneiform tablet, dated 2100–2000 B.C.E., records an early business transaction.**

found with him, and photographs of the site, the body, details of artifacts, and a map locating the site.

The growth of empires is illustrated with an outstanding collection of artifacts, including pottery and stone tools from Troy, Luristan bronzes, a Cycladic figurine, Etruscan bronzes, Greek pottery, Roman glass, a Roman mosaic, and Roman money.

By about A.D. 500, the basic patterns of Western culture were set, and many of them persist today. A section of the hall focuses on present-day life with a reconstructed modern bazaar scene. A Roman cookbook is compared with a modern one.

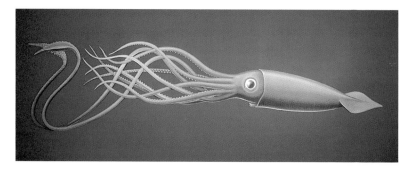

Visitors to "In Search of Giant Squid" can learn about the elusive giant squid and see an artist's rendering of what it would look like.

## IN SEARCH OF GIANT SQUID

No one has yet to see a giant squid alive in its natural habitat. But the search continues, and over the last decade museum scientist Dr. Clyde F. E. Roper has devoted his career to the pursuit of the elusive giant squid—*Architeuthis* sp. This exhibit highlights the most recent efforts by Dr. Roper to locate living giant squid in New Zealand waters—a hotbed of activity for giant squid specimens. A video and an introductory kiosk update the ecological and biological information known about the giant squid. Two squid specimens are on display—a 30-foot-long giant squid, *Architeuthis dux,* and a large oceanic squid, *Taningia danae,* nearly nine feet in length (a world record for this species), with eyes as big as grapefruits, and claws along the length of her eight arms. Visitors learn that squid are the largest invertebrates in the world, a

member of the mollusk family. Myths about giant squid are dispelled, as scientific data reveal facts that are even more fascinating than the fiction.

## BONES

Hundreds of skeletons of mammals, birds, reptiles, amphibians, and fishes, ranging from the gigantic extinct Steller sea cow to the tiny pocket mouse, are shown in characteristic poses and grouped by order to illustrate their relationships. Exhibits show how bone structures evolved in adaptation to environment. Horses, for example, developed leg and foot bones that enabled them to run swiftly on the level grasslands where they lived and grazed. The skeleton of a famous racehorse, Lexington (1850–75), illustrates this adaptation.

## REPTILES

The subtropical Florida Everglades—home of alligators, tree frogs, turtles, and a variety of snakes, including the diamondback rattlesnake—is one of the life-size habitat displays in this hall. The king cobra, reticulated python, and boa constrictors from the Malayan and Amazonian jungle are among the large snakes on view. Feeding habitats, locomotion methods, and the influence of human economics on reptiles and amphibians are also illustrated.

**The massive skeleton of a Stellar sea cow—perhaps the most complete such skeleton in existence—looms over skeletons of other meat-eating animals. It was assembled from bones salvaged on Bering Island in 1883.**

AT A GLANCE

Dinosaurs, the Hope diamond, the African bush elephant, Native American objects, and the O. Orkin Insect Zoo are among the most popular features of this museum. Also of special interest are the Discovery Room, where visitors of all ages can touch, feel, smell, and taste a variety of natural specimens, and the exhibition "Life in the Ancient Seas."

### O. ORKIN INSECT ZOO

The whirls, chirps, buzzes, and rattles heard at the entrance to this hall are the sounds of the most abundant, diverse, and successful animals on Earth—insects and their relatives. One of the most popular attractions in the insect zoo is the walk-through tropical rainforest, with live giant cockroaches that in nature would dwell in the forest litter and tree hollows. Also in the rainforest are cave arthropods and other invertebrates. Caves teem with life forms that are attracted to year-round constant temperature and moisture.

The interactive exhibits and participatory activities in the insect zoo invite exploration and involvement by visitors of all ages. Children can crawl through a large model of an African termite mound, look into a real beehive, or touch a giant grasshopper. Visitors can hold some of the more docile animals in the zoo. Docents are available to answer questions. The popular tarantula feedings take place several times a day.

### FORCES OF CHANGES

At the exit to the IMAX® theater is a hall devoted to the study of geological, biological, and cultural change. "Forces of Change" is a program under development at the museum about the dynamics of global change. By integrating expertise from all the disciplines of the museum's scientific community, "Forces of Change" demonstrates how understanding the concept of change is central to understanding our world.

This pioneering program will help visitors see the connection between topics as seemingly remote as gas bubbled within the Antarctic ice cap and famines in tropical Africa.

Through exhibits, publications, computer products, and a variety of public programs, "Forces of Change" is dedicated to exploring the forces that shape and sustain our world. The program includes plans for a 6,000-square-foot permanent exhibit, a companion book, and exhibits that open at the museum and travel to museums, science centers, and libraries across the country. "Global Links," a multimedia display that integrates satellite imagery with museum collections to tell stories about dynamic Earth processes is currently on exhibit in the hall.

Above: The bite of most tarantula species is no more dangerous to humans than a bee sting. Left: Leaf-cutter ants from the O. Orkin Insect Zoo. Opposite: The entrance to the O. Orkin Insect Zoo, where visitors can touch and hold live insects. Overleaf: A glass elevator in the Discovery Center takes visitors to the Samuel C. Johnson Theater showing 2-D and 3-D IMAX® films.

Near the Mall and Constitution Avenue entrances. There is also an electronic information kiosk by the museum stores on the ground floor.

## TOURS

Guided public walk-in tours are given daily at 10:30 A.M. and 1:30 P.M., September through June. Confirm tour times at information desks or call 202-357-2700, or 202-357-1729 (TTY). Self-guided audio tours are available in the Rotunda on the first floor.

## ACCESS

The Mall entrance is not accessible to visitors in wheelchairs and those who cannot climb stairs readily. Most museum services are accessible to visitors with disabilities. Loop amplifications are available in the center front rows of Baird Auditorium. For special services for groups, call 202-786-2178, or 202-633-9287 (TTY); or fax to 202-786-2778. To receive the museum's calendar of events, call 202-357-4014, or 202-633-9287 (TTY).

## WHERE TO EAT

The Atrium Café in the Discovery Center on the ground floor offers hamburgers, hot dogs, French fries, pizza, roast chicken, pasta, submarine sandwiches, salads, ice cream, desserts, beverages, and other lunch items in a casual atmosphere. The Fossil Café in the dinosaur complex on the first floor offers espresso, lattes, cookies, muffins, salads, and light snacks.

## MUSEUM STORE

The main museum store on the ground floor carries a variety of Smithsonian souvenirs and gifts related to natural history, including a wide selection of jewelry, books, cassette tapes, and compact discs. Across the hall is a store especially appealing to children. Theme-oriented shops elsewhere in the museum feature books and memorabilia relating to permanent and special exhibitions.

## DISCOVERY ROOM

This special area on the first floor is a family-oriented, flexible education facility featuring multisensory experiences with objects from the world of nature. Hours are Monday through Thursday, 12 noon to 2:30 P.M.; Friday, Saturday, and Sunday, 10:30 A.M. to 3:30 p.m. Free passes are distributed daily at the room's entrance. Groups of more than five are not admitted during regular hours. One adult must accompany every two to three children. For a group reservation application form, call 202-357-2747, or 202-633-9287 (TTY), or fax to 202-786-2778.

## FILMS

Check the museum's Web site or call 202-633-7400 for schedules and ticketing information for the Johnson IMAX® Theater and Immersion Cinema.

## PARDON OUR DUST

Exhibitions are subject to change owing to renovations and restorations of the halls. The Discovery Room is scheduled to move to the Discovery Center at an unspecified date.

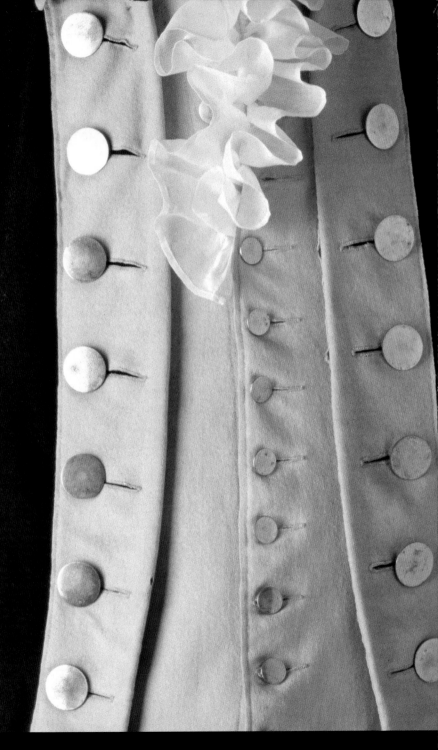

Above: General George Washington began wearing this uniform coat around 1789, after he had resigned from the Continental Army to become the nation's commander-in-chief. Opposite top: The "Teddy bear" was created by the Ideal Toy Company and named after Theodore Roosevelt in 1903.

# NATIONAL MUSEUM OF AMERICAN HISTORY,

## BEHRING CENTER

Constitution Avenue between 12th and 14th Streets, NW. Mall entrance: Madison Drive between 12th and 14th Streets, NW. Open daily, except December 25, 10 A.M. to 5:30 P.M. Metrorail: Federal Triangle or Smithsonian station. Smithsonian information: 202-357-2700 TTY: 202-357-1729. HistoryWired.si.edu americanhistory.si.edu

In 1858, the "objects of art and of foreign and curious research" in the National Cabinet of Curiosities were transferred from the U.S. Patent Office to the Smithsonian Institution. This was the genesis of the collections in the National Museum of American History, Behring Center. After the Centennial Exposition of 1876 closed, the Smithsonian received a windfall of objects that had been displayed in Philadelphia for the nation's 100th anniversary celebration. Many of those objects were put on exhibit in the U.S. National Museum Building (now the Arts and Industries Building) when it opened in 1881. Today, the spacious halls of the National Museum of American History are filled with exhibits that explore America's social, cultural, scientific, and technological history.

Top: This teapot, tray, and document box are made of tin-plated sheet iron known as tinware. Bottom: This Art Deco bracelet and brooch of 1940 are made of 14-karat gold, aquamarines, diamonds, and rubies.

## FIRST FLOOR

### COUNTRY STORE POST OFFICE

Adjacent to the Constitution Avenue entrance is a country store that was located in Headsville, West Virginia, from the 1860s to 1971, serving as a post office about half those years. Brought to the museum lock, stock, and barrel (staples and sundries of a bygone era still line the shelves), it again functions as an official post office. Stamps, including special issues, may be purchased here, and mail that is deposited receives a unique, hand-stamped "Smithsonian Station" postmark.

### A MATERIAL WORLD

The materials that compose an object can reveal a great deal about the people who made and used it—about their environment, skills, and values. This exhibition introduces materials that make up objects of everyday life and helps visitors think about other objects in the museum in new ways.

## FARM MACHINES

A wooden plow from colonial times can be compared with later steel plows, the traditional cradle scythe and winnowing fan with a 20-mule-team Holt combine of 1886. The International Harvester cotton harvester ("Old Red") of 1943 symbolizes the transformation of the labor-intensive cotton culture to one dominated by machines. The internal-combustion tractors illustrate major developments, from the 1918 Waterloo Boy to the 1924 John Deere and a more-recent International Harvester. The exhibition is scheduled to close in 2002.

## AMERICA ON THE MOVE

In 2002, construction will begin on "America on the Move," a new permanent exhibition about the history of transportation in America from 1876 to 2000.

**The 1918 Waterloo Boy, which ran on kerosene, was one of the most widely used tractors of its day.**

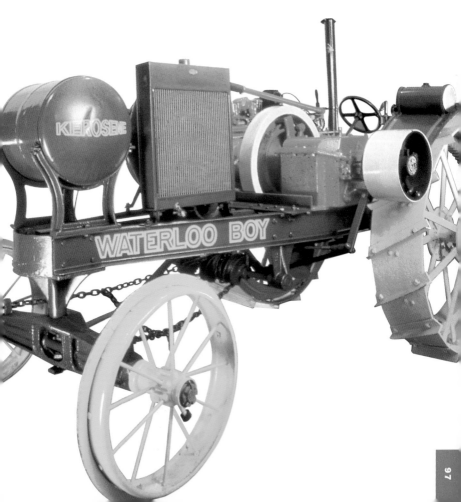

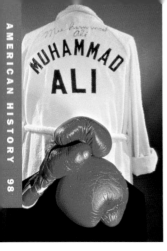

## AT A GLANCE

The Star-Spangled Banner, the First Ladies' gowns, Abraham Lincoln's hat, Lewis and Clark's compass, Muhammad Ali's boxing gloves, Thomas Jefferson's wooden lap desk on which he wrote the Declaration of Independence, the John Bull locomotive, Kermit the Frog—the list of America's favorites could go on and on in this wide-ranging, entertaining, and educational museum.

The exhibition will highlight the museum's unparalleled and extremely popular transportation collections in new and creative ways. Using multimedia technology and engaging case studies, "America on the Move" will bring the museum's trains, trucks, ships, and automobiles back to life—or, more accurately, back to history. For the first time, visitors will be able to see the artifacts as they once were: moving people and products from place to place. A vital part of the nation's transportation system, they were also central to American business, social, and cultural history. The exhibition is expected to open by 2004.

### AMERICAN MARITIME ENTERPRISE

Using the Smithsonian's National Watercraft Collection, founded in 1884, this permanent exhibition chronicles the broad sweep of our nation's ocean and river commerce from the *Mayflower* to the present day. Highlights include a *Titanic* life vest, the earliest-known American marine steam engine, the original builder's model of a mid-19th-century African American whale ship, World War II *Liberty* and *Victory* ship models, and a tattoo parlor. The exhibition is expected to close in late 2002 for the construction of "America on the Move" and will reopen by 2004, concurrent with that exhibition.

### POWER MACHINERY

The full-size engines and models displayed here illustrate the harnessing of atmospheric forces, the early age of steam power, and the development of high-pressure and high-speed engines. Exhibits show the evolution of steam boilers and the steam turbine, and progress in the techniques of harnessing waterpower. The collection also includes a number of historic internal-combustion engines.

## LIGHTING A REVOLUTION

Thomas Edison's revolutionary invention is only the beginning of the story of electricity, which is the subject of this exhibition. Here, visitors can explore the similarities and differences between the process of invention in Edison's era and today.

## ON TIME

This exhibition looks at the changing ways Americans have measured, used, and thought about time during the past 300 years. It aims to stimulate visitors to think about time, both in American history and in their own lives, in new ways. In addition to almost 200 clocks, watches, and other timekeeping devices, the exhibition—including an "Open

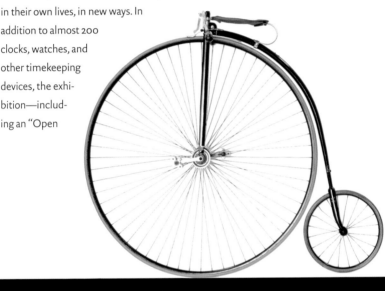

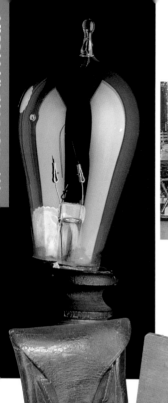

24 Hours" neon sign illuminating America's around-the-clock culture—features certain "landmark" objects to reveal how perceptions of time have changed.

### ENGINES OF CHANGE: THE AMERICAN INDUSTRIAL REVOLUTION, 1790–1860

With more than 250 original artifacts, this major exhibition brings to life the American Industrial Revolution. It tells the stories of craftspeople, factory workers, inventors, and entrepreneurs who transformed America from an agricultural to an industrial society.

The Slater spinning frame, the world's oldest operable locomotive (the *John Bull*), and the Colt revolver are among the objects that illustrate the ingenuity of the age and the effects of industrialization on American life.

### SCIENCE IN AMERICAN LIFE

In modern America, science and society are inseparable. Over the last 125 years, scientific research and science-based technology have been the most powerful agents of change in American life, and science has grown into a complex enterprise interwoven with all aspects of our culture. Through artifacts, historical photographs, and multimedia technology, this exhibition focuses on many of the scientific issues, achievements, misunderstandings, and controversies that have shaped contemporary life.

**Top left: A Thomas Edison lightbulb, early 1880. Top right: Built in England in 1831, the *John Bull* is the oldest operable locomotive in the world. Bottom: Lewis and Clark used this compass (with case) on their expedition to the unchartered northwest territory in 1804–6.**

To help visitors understand how science works and discover how science and society interact, the Hands On Science Center invites them to learn science by doing. Visitors can solve a crime using DNA finger-printing methods, test for food additives and water purity, learn what type of a "gas" carbon dioxide is, use a Geiger counter to test for radioactivity in everyday objects, experiment with different methods to clean up an oil spill, discover the many ways plastics can be reused, and find out the ultraviolet rating for their sunglasses. Working alone or with the center's staff, visitors ages 5 and older learn the principles underlying these technologies as they experience the fun and excitement of experimental science.

Section of the Electrical Numerical Integrator and Computer (ENIAC), which in 1945 helped launch the computer industry. The ENIAC, taking up an entire room, weighed 30 tons and used 18,000 vacuum tubes.

INFORMATION AGE: PEOPLE, INFORMATION, AND TECHNOLOGY

Beginning with Samuel Morse's invention of the telegraph in the 1830s, this exhibition explores how information technology has changed our lives—as individuals and as a society—over the past 150 years. Objects such as Morse's telegraph, a piece of the first transatlantic telegraph cable, Alexander Graham Bell's original telephone, the early ENIAC computer, and modern microcomputers are on display. The exhibition also looks at the influence of radio, television, wartime advances in information technology, the rise of the computer industry, and the spread of computer use into many sectors of modern life.

## SECOND FLOOR

### CEREMONIAL COURT

A White House welcome awaits visitors to the Ceremonial Court as they enter the re-created Cross Hall of the Executive Mansion. Dating from the 1902 renovation during Theodore Roosevelt's presidency, the original furnishings seen here include crystal chandeliers, enormous mirrors, mantels, pilasters, and plasterwork. Adjoining galleries showcase outstanding items from the national collections and presidential memorabilia. On view are examples of White House china from George Washington's Chinese export porcelain to more recent patterns, and fine examples of American art glass, jewelry, red earthenware, silver, stoneware, and painted tinware.

**Top and middle: Presidential campaign memorabilia, 1950s–60s. Bottom: White House china from Lyndon B. Johnson's administration. Opposite: The wife of the mayor of New York wore this gown to George Washington's inaugural ball in 1789.**

### FIRST LADIES: POLITICAL ROLE AND PUBLIC IMAGE

Since the time of Martha Washington, First Ladies have fascinated the American people. This exhibition explores the responsibilities of presidential wives and hostesses and examines how the role of the First Lady has evolved into one of international celebrity and recognized political power. Historical photographs, documentary film, period graphics, campaign items,

**Above: The First Ladies exhibition features a selection of 20th-century inaugural gowns. Right: Lady Bird Johnson's inaugural gown, 1965.**

gowns, and other personal artifacts help the visitor trace the individual social and political accomplishments of the First Lady while underscoring her traditional responsibilities. The museum's renowned First Ladies' gown collection is the centerpiece of this area.

### FROM PARLOR TO POLITICS: WOMEN AND REFORM IN AMERICA, 1890–1925

The expansion of women's roles in shaping public policy is the focus of this exhibition. Organized around three domestic spaces—a parlor, a tenement, and Jane Addams's Hull House settlement in Chicago—it examines how women used the images and language of their homemaking and child-rearing roles as a rationale for participating in political reform movements.

## PRESERVING THE STAR-SPANGLED BANNER: THE FLAG THAT INSPIRED THE NATIONAL ANTHEM

The museum is home to the Star-Spangled Banner, the flag that inspired the words to the national anthem. In this space, visitors learn about the flag's history and its ongoing preservation. Specially designed floor-to-ceiling windows allow the visitor to view the progress of the flag's treatment in the adjacent conservation lab.

Conservators preserving the Star-Spangled Banner—the flag that in 1814 inspired Francis Scott Key to pen the poem that would become the national anthem.

## AFTER THE REVOLUTION: EVERYDAY LIFE IN AMERICA, 1780–1800

"After the Revolution" illuminates the lives of families and communities in the 1780s and 1790s. Moving from rural to urban settings, the exhibition concentrates on the Delaware farm family of Thomas and Elizabeth Springer and their two daughters; African Americans in the Chesapeake area; the Virginia planter family of Henry and Ann Saunders and their daughter Betsy; the Seneca nation of the Iroquois Confederacy; the

Massachusetts merchant family of Samuel and Lucy Colton; and the major urban center of Philadelphia.

### FIELD TO FACTORY: AFRO-AMERICAN MIGRATION, 1915–1940

Between 1915 and 1940, more than one million African Americans left the South and headed north in search of a better life. This great migration was carried out by ordinary people making individual choices. "Field to Factory" looks at the hardships of southern life and its

strengths; at the personal decisions to leave; and at city life in the North, where jobs were often menial and housing overcrowded but where new communities and new racial pride emerged. The exhibition features a Maryland sharecropper's house of about 1920; a replica of the separate entrances for whites and blacks at the Ashland, Virginia, train station; objects from a beauty salon run by Marjorie Stewart Joyner, one of the new black business owners; and a re-creation of a city row house.

**Above and opposite: The story of a sharecropping family introduces "Field to Factory," which explores the massive migration of African Americans from the rural South to the urban North between about 1915 and 1940.**

"Communities in a Changing Nation" examines the promise of America in the 1800s through the experiences of three different communities. Visitors will walk through the industrial era in Bridgeport, Connecticut;

The flag of the 84th Regiment U.S. Colored Infantry lists areas in Louisiana and Texas where the men fought in many Civil War campaigns.

relive the Jewish immigrant experience in Cincinnati, Ohio; and witness slavery and freedom among African Americans in Charleston, South Carolina.

### WITHIN THESE WALLS . . .

"Within These Walls . . ." tells the history of a house that stood at 16 Elm Street in Ipswich, Massachusetts, and five of the many families who occupied it from the mid-1760s through 1945. The exhibition explores some of the important ways ordinary people, in their daily lives, have been part of the great changes and events in American history. The centerpiece is the largest artifact in the museum, a Georgian-style, 2 1/2–story timber-framed house built in the 1760s, saved from the bulldozer by the citizens of Ipswich in 1963, and relo-

cated to this space within the museum. Within this house from Ipswich, American colonists created new ways of living, patriots sparked a Revolution, an African American struggled for freedom, community activists organized to end slavery, immigrants built new identities for themselves, and a grandmother and her grandson served on the home front during World War II.

### AMERICAN ENCOUNTERS

The arrival of Columbus in the Americas in 1492 began a series of global encounters between peoples of Africa, Asia, Europe, and the Americas that have in large part shaped the modern world. This exhibition focuses on one of those encounters that continues today and the creative ways in which the people living in what is now New Mexico's Upper Rio Grande Valley have preserved their cultures. The encounter began in 1539, when Zuni Indians discovered representatives of

A 2 1/2–story timber-framed house from 1760 (top left) was brought to the museum from Ipswich, Massachusetts, in 1963 and is the centerpiece of the exhibition "Within These Walls . . ." (top right). Bottom: Dolls like this one, made in England in the 1700s, helped little girls from the wealthiest families learn to dress like ladies.

## SMITHSONIAN INSTITUTION LIBRARIES GALLERY

The Smithsonian Institution Libraries Gallery—separately administered from the National Museum of American History but located on the museum's first floor (look for signs to "Dibner Gallery")—is home to the annual exhibitions of the Smithsonian Institution Libraries. Exhibitions, which are thematic, feature books and special collections from the Libraries' extensive, multifaceted holdings and are organized by guest curators from around the Institution. For more information, see page 20.

**Above: These late-19th-century examples are among the 40,000 rare books in the collections of the Smithsonian Institution Libraries. Right: On display in "Communities in a Changing Nation: The Promise of 19th-Century America," this suit of armor was originally purchased around 1880 by Benjamin B. Comegys, a Philadelphia banker, for his library.**

the Spanish government seeking gold, silver, and souls in their land. It continued with the arrival of Anglo Americans to the region in the early 1800s. Among the artifacts on view are pottery and trade goods from the Puye and Santa Clara Indian cultures, religious artifacts such as crosses, altars, and costumes, and Hispanic blankets and weaving equipment.

### HANDS ON HISTORY ROOM

More than 30 activities built around reproductions of historical artifacts offer visitors a chance to touch, examine, and use objects similar to those elsewhere in the museum. This is the place for everyone—adults and children ages 5 and older—to learn by doing. Activities include pedaling a high-wheeler, sending a message by telegraph, turning the handle of a cotton gin, plucking and striking keyboard instruments from the

18th and 19th centuries, and studying the designs and symbols on Zuni and Santa Clara pots, then decorating a paper one. Young children especially will enjoy Betsy's Moving Trunk, which lets them unpack the trunk of a little girl from a Virginia plantation and learn about life in the 1780s.

## THIRD FLOOR
### ARMED FORCES HISTORY
Uniforms, weapons, paintings, and flags illustrate the origin and growth of the armed forces and the life of the citizen soldier. Highlights include George Washington's field-headquarters tent and a Revolutionary War vessel—the Continental gunboat *Philadelphia*—dating from 1776.

**The Continental fleet's gunboat *Philadelphia*, which sank in battle in 1776, was discovered and raised from Lake Champlain in 1935.**

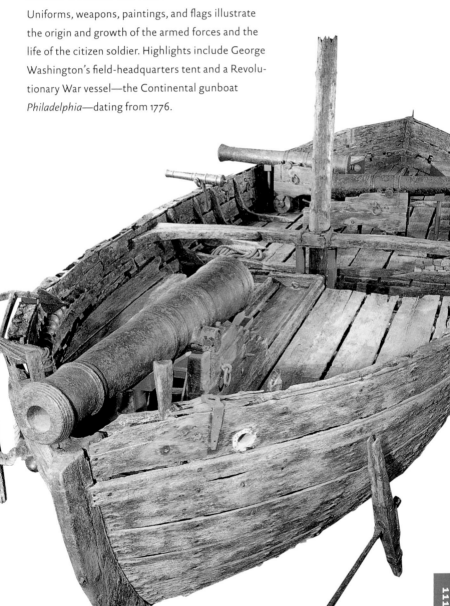

"Defend Your Country"
recruiting poster, 1940s.

WORLD WAR II G.I.: THE AMERICAN
SOLDIER'S EXPERIENCE

The experiences of the average citizen-soldier of
World War II, also known as "G.I.," for Government
Issue, are examined in this exhibition. Forever changed
from the naive, insular teenager of the 1940s, the
American G.I. was shaped overnight, together with his
Army and his country, into a modern military force.

## FAST ATTACKS AND BOOMERS: SUBMARINES IN THE COLD WAR

Nuclear-powered submarines played major roles in American policy and strategy from the 1950s to the 1990s, the years of the Cold War between the United States and the Soviet Union. This exhibition explores the technology of submarines and their role in the Cold War. It also showcases life aboard ship through graphics, interactives, and artifacts from decommissioned ships, and examines the role of Navy families.

## PERSONAL LEGACY: THE HEALING OF A NATION

This thought-provoking installation commemorates the Vietnam Veterans Memorial located near the Lincoln Memorial in Washington, D.C. The exhibition includes some 500 items from a collection of more than 25,000 objects deposited at the memorial between 1982 and October 31, 1991. On display are flags, memorial wreaths, stuffed toy animals, dog tags, military insignia, combat medals, battle jackets, and personal letters as well as a scale model of the memorial.

## A MORE PERFECT UNION: JAPANESE AMERICANS AND THE U.S. CONSTITUTION

In the early weeks of World War II, the U.S. government forced some 120,000 people of Japanese ancestry to leave their homes and go to detention camps for the duration of the war. Two-thirds were American citizens, and their rights and privileges under the Constitution were swept away. All were considered security risks. This exhibition looks at prewar prejudice against Japanese Americans; the evacuation and relocation of men, women, and children; life in the camps; Japanese American troops defending the nation in combat; and Japanese Americans' efforts since the war to prevent another wholesale loss of liberties for themselves and others.

Johnnie V. Wilson of Council Bluffs, Iowa, wore these metal identification badges during World War II. So-called dog tags are used to identify a soldier wounded or killed in action.

## THE AMERICAN PRESIDENCY: A GLORIOUS BURDEN

"The American Presidency: A Glorious Burden" looks at the personal, public, ceremonial, and executive actions of the men who have held this office and impacted the course of history in the past 200 years. More than 900 artifacts, including national treasures from the Smithsonian's vast presidential collections, bring to life the role of the presidency in American culture. Among the exhibition's highlights are Thomas Jefferson's wooden lap desk on which he wrote the Declaration of Independence; the carriage Ulysses S. Grant rode to his second inauguration; the top hat worn by Abraham Lincoln the night of his assassination; George Washington's battle sword; Bill Clinton's military case used to contain the topmost national security information; a 1999 script from the TV drama *The West Wing;* and the suit worn by Harrison Ford in the 1997 movie *Air Force One.*

**Top: Thomas Jefferson drafted the Declaration of Independence on this lap desk. Above: One of the Smithsonian's treasured icons is the top hat worn by Abraham Lincoln to Ford's Theatre on the night of his assassination, April 15, 1865. Right: Franklin D. Roosevelt used this microphone for his "fireside chats."**

## PRINTING AND GRAPHIC ARTS

This hall deals with the history of prints and printing techniques. Settings feature a printing office of Benjamin Franklin's time, with two wooden presses; a 19th-century foundry in which type was still cast by hand, as it had been since Gutenberg's day, and a job shop of 1865, equipped with a hand-and-treadle press.

The "Digilab" offers a unique behind-the-scenes view into the applications of modern technology, allowing visitors to view the scanning of objects and photographs to create 3-D digital images, Web sites, and other digital archives. The companion exhibition considers how digitization is changing the printing industry and the technology for graphic arts.

## MONEY AND MEDALS

The story that unfolds here centers on the evolution of monetary exchange. A special feature is the gold room. In addition to coinage and currency from many nations, the hall includes a coin collector's browsing area.

Top: John Trumbull's portrait of Martha Washington, 1795. Bottom: William Howard Taft's inaugural souvenir plate, 1909.

**Right: Prince designed his Yellow Cloud guitar, 1989. Opposite: The museum has one of the finest collections of Stradivarius instruments, which are used regularly in performances around the world. This detail shows the stenciling on the famed Axelrod Quartet.**

## ICONS OF AMERICAN POPULAR CULTURE

This exhibition gathers together widely recognized artifacts of American popular culture, including the ruby slippers worn by Dorothy in the 1939 movie *The Wizard of Oz*, Michael Jordan's jersey worn during the 1996–97 National Basketball Association season, Dizzy Gillespie's trumpet, a *Star Trek* phaser used on the popular NBC TV series from 1966 to 1969, Arthur Ashe's 1975 tennis racket, Muhammad Ali's boxing gloves from the championship fight with George Foreman in 1974, and Indiana Jones's jacket and hat, among other items.

## MUSICAL INSTRUMENTS

Displayed in a setting that includes an intimate hall used for concerts and recordings, these instruments are exquisite examples of Western European and American craftsmanship. Some have been carefully restored to playing condition. In addition to a permanent display of organs, harpsichords, and pianos, changing exhibits of stringed, wind, and percussion instruments represent various musical traditions.

## TEXTILES

Clothmaking in the American colonies was an arduous process involving the transformation of raw flax and wool into finished fabrics for clothing and household goods. A variety of 19th-century American implements for making textiles

are on display here. Rarities include a hand-operated
knitting frame from the 1700s and a French Jacquard–
equipped loom of the 1840s. Shawls, coverlets, hand
embroideries of the 18th and 19th centuries,
Jacquard-woven coverlets and pictures, and other
fine examples of historic textiles from the museum
collections are featured.

**Following pages: Jim
Henson's Kermit the
Frog, 1970 (p. 118). The
Palm Court creates a
19th-century ambiance
(p. 119).**

W.BAK
DORCHES
MASS. NO.
CHOCOLATE
Premium
12 1-Lb. Pkgs. (Halves)
12 Lbs Net
WALTER
Paris Expos
Keep co

Near the Mall and Constitution Avenue entrances

For information on concerts, lectures, films, and other activities, inquire at the information desks.

Tours include Highlights, Field to Factory, and First Ladies' Gowns. Schedules vary seasonally. Demonstrations include interpretive carts illustrating the Cotton Gin, Early Recorded Sound, and Electricity; Power Machinery; Printing and Graphic Arts; and 1776 (the story of the Revolutionary War gunboat *Philadelphia*). In the Hands On History Room, visitors handle reproductions of historical artifacts, and in the Hands On Science Center, visitors participate in experiments. Ask at the information desks for current times and topics, or call 202-357-2700, or 202-357-1729 (TTY). For special school and adult tours, call 202-357-1481, or 202-357-1563 (TTY), Monday through Friday.

A cafeteria is located on the lower level. The Palm Court on the first floor serves ice cream and light refreshments.

For sale in the museum store on the lower level are a wide variety of objects and publications relating to American history and civilization, together with postcards, slides, film, T-shirts, and posters. Two smaller museum stores including one devoted to music are located at the Mall entrance.

In 2002, the museum begins major renovation to all exhibition floors. Some artifacts and exhibitions pictured and described in this guide may be removed or relocated. Current schedules are available at the information desks and on our Web site americanhistory.si.edu.

Above: Frieze showing four scenes from the life of a Buddha, carved in high relief of seven pieces of dark gray-blue slate. Pakistan, Kushan dynasty (A.D. 50–200), late 2d–early 3d century A.D. Opposite: *White Avalokiteshvara*, Nepal, ca. 14th century, wood with pigment

Independence Avenue
(accessible entrance)
at 12th Street, SW.
Mall entrance:
Jefferson Drive
at 12th Street, SW.
Open daily, except
December 25,
10 A.M. to 5:30 P.M.
Metrorail:
Smithsonian station.
Smithsonian
information:
202-357-2700
TTY: 202-357-1729.
www.asia.si.edu

# FREER GALLERY OF ART

The Freer Gallery of Art opened in 1923 as the first national museum of fine arts. Its collection of Asian art is internationally preeminent. Produced over six millennia, the Asian collections represent the creative traditions of China, Japan, Korea, South and Southeast Asia, and the West and includes examples of ancient Egyptian and early Christian art. Its select 19th- and early 20th-century American art boasts the world's largest and most important group of works by James McNeill Whistler (1834–1903). Because only a small part of the permanent collection can be shown at one time, changing selections of art are presented on a rotating schedule.

Charles Lang Freer (1854–1919), a Detroit industrialist, founded the museum; its unusual combination of creative tradi-

The Freer Gallery of Art has one of the finest collections of Asian art in the world. These magnificent holdings, which span Neolithic times to the early 20th century, share exhibition space in the Italian Renaissance–style building with a major group of 19th- and early 20th-century American art. The Freer Gallery houses the world's most comprehensive collection of works by James McNeill Whistler, including *Harmony in Blue and Gold: The Peacock Room,* the artist's only existing interior design scheme, permanently installed in the Freer.

tions—Asian and American—reflect his unique preference. Freer began collecting American art in the 1880s. He limited his acquisitions to the work of a few living artists and concentrated especially on Whistler. He began collecting Asian art in 1887 and had assembled a collection of Asian masterpieces by the time of his death in 1919. Freer once wrote that he attempted to "gather together objects of art covering various periods of production, all of which are harmonious and allied in many ways."

In his bequest to the nation, Freer gave 7,500 Asian paintings, sculptures, and drawings, as well as works of calligraphy, metal, lacquer, and jade. Many other generous donors have since participated in the growth of the Asian collection, which now num-

bers 26,500 objects. Freer asked that his American collection remain as he presented it, with some 1,500 works by artists whom he knew personally and whose work he admired. The American collection has long been an inspiration for original research by scholars from many nations.

Freer also donated the funds for a building in which to house his collection. He believed the Italian Renaissance style would provide an appropriate setting for the display of his art, and he worked closely on the plans for the building with architect Charles A. Platt. The loggias, or open galleries that surround the gracious Italianate courtyard, enable visitors to enjoy views of beautiful plantings as well as bronze sculptures, which adorn the area. Today, the building is on the National Register of Historic Places. The Freer Gallery of Art is connected by an underground exhibition space to the Arthur M. Sackler Gallery, also a Smithsonian museum of Asian art.

Above: A detail of the northeast corner of *Harmony in Blue and Gold: The Peacock Room*, the only existing interior design scheme by James McNeill Whistler (American, 1834–1903) and an icon of the Freer Gallery of Art. Opposite top: Whistler's *Variations in Flesh Colour and Green: The Balcony*, 1864–70, oil on wood panel. Opposite bottom: Jar, Korea, Chosen period, Yi dynasty, ca. 1900, glazed porcelain clay.

Above: Katsushika Hokusai, *Boy Viewing Mount Fuji*, Japan, Edo period, ca. 1839, ink and color on silk. Right: Den Shiru (1743–1805), *Geomantic Verdit from the I-Ching*, hanging scroll, ink on paper. Opposite: The courtyard, Freer Gallery of Art.

Ongoing exhibitions include American art, Japanese art, Korean ceramics, Chinese painting, Whistler's *Harmony in Blue and Gold: The Peacock Room*, ancient Chinese art, Buddhist art, South Asian art, Islamic art, Egyptian glass, and "Luxury Arts of the Silk Route Empires." A variety of free public lectures, concerts, films, and other programs complement the exhibitions.

## ENTRANCES

The main visitors' entrance is located on Jefferson Drive, SW. The street-level entrance on Independence Avenue has elevator service to the galleries. The Arthur M. Sackler Gallery is accessible through an underground gallery.

## INFORMATION DESK

In the lobby near the Jefferson Drive entrance

## TOURS

Free guided tours are given daily at specific times. Confirm walk-in tour times at the information desk or call 202-357-2700, or 202-357-1729 (TTY). Request special group tours in writing at least four weeks in advance. Write to: Tours, Freer Gallery of Art, Smithsonian Institution, Washington, D.C. 20560-0707.

## GALLERY SHOP

Museum reproductions, books, posters, prints, jewelry, cards, and gifts related to the collections are for sale in the shop on the Freer's second level.

## LIBRARY

A library serving the Freer and Sackler Galleries is located in the Sackler. It has nearly 60,000 volumes, about half of which are in Chinese and Japanese, and subscribes to more than 400 periodicals. Researchers may examine the more than 100,000 photographic images in the archives. About 73,000 slides are available for loan. Library hours are 10 A.M. to 5 P.M., Monday through Friday. Appointments are necessary; call 202-357-4880.

Above: *Portrait of Yinti, Prince Xun, and Wife* (detail), China, Qing dynasty, 2d half 18th century, hanging scroll, ink and color on silk. Opposite top: Tomb guardian, China, Tang

1050 Independence
Avenue, SW.
Entered from Enid A.
Haupt Garden through
ground-level pavilion.
Open daily, except
December 25,
10 A.M. to 5:30 P.M.
Metrorail:
Smithsonian station.
Smithsonian
information:
202-357-2700
TTY: 202-357-1729.
www.asia.si.edu

# ARTHUR M. SACKLER GALLERY

Founded in 1987 with a group of 1,000
masterpieces of Asian art given by Arthur
M. Sackler, M.D. (1913–1987), the Sackler
Gallery is a leader in educating the public
about a continent that plays an ever-larger
role in the lives of Americans. The museum explores Asia's distinctive traditions
in a varied program of exhibitions from its
own collection and others in the United
States and abroad. Archaeological riches
lend variety to presentations from different centuries and geographic areas, including art, crafts, and design in many media.

Exhibitions of work by living artists
have included such diverse examples as
animal paintings by a young Chinese girl,
baskets by an 80-year-old craftsman from
rural Japan, installation art from a Chinese calligrapher, and a nine-foot-tall

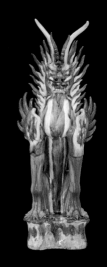

**Album page, *A Demon Descends on a Horseman*, Iran, ca. 1550, opaque watercolor and gold on paper.**

fiberglass work by an Indian sculptor. Some exhibitions and docent-led tours offer visitors the opportunity to touch objects and feel their weight and texture. A selection of porcelain masterworks by contemporary Japanese artists, for example, included pottery shards for visitors to handle. Reading areas furnished with educational materials are often incorporated into exhibition designs.

Programs of film, music, dance, and drama present a broad survey of Asian culture. Outdoor dance and music performances attract crowds to the art inside. Members of local Asian communities often advise on and participate in the gallery's public programs. Regular public lectures reinforce themes intro-

Above: Sahiba Ram (1740–1800), fragment from a larger work showing Maharaja Pratap Singh with ladies of the royal harem, India, ca. late 18th century, opaque watercolor, silver, and gold on paper. Left: Rhyton, Iran, Sasanian period, A.D. 300–400, silver and gilt.

## AT A GLANCE

The Arthur M. Sackler Gallery houses an important gift of Asian art from Arthur M. Sackler, M.D. (1913–1987). Exhibitions from the permanent collection as well as international presentations from Japan, China, Indonesia, Korea, India, Sri Lanka, and other nations trace the development of Asian and Near Eastern art from ancient times to the present.

duced in the exhibitions or complement those topics with presentations of related research.

The Sackler Gallery involves families through its popular "Imagin-Asia," a program of hands-on activities that encourage families to explore an exhibition and create a related project to take home. The workshops begin in the classroom on the second level. Themes and times vary and include weekends. For more information, call 202-357-2700.

## ENTRANCE

Enter from Independence Avenue through a ground-level pavilion and proceed to exhibition areas on two lower levels. The Freer Gallery of Art, with related exhibitions and programs, is accessible by an underground gallery.

## INFORMATION DESK

In the entrance pavilion

## TOURS

Free guided tours are given daily at specific times. Confirm walk-in tour times at the information desk or call 202-357-2700, or 202-357-1729 (TTY). Request special group tours in writing at least four weeks in advance. Write to: Tours, Arthur M. Sackler Gallery, Smithsonian Institution, Washington, D.C. 20560-0707.

## GALLERY SHOP

The shop, located on the first level, features quality merchandise based on the museum's collections and Asian cultures. Porcelain, crafts, jewelry, textiles, books, prints, and cards are available.

## LIBRARY

A library serving the Freer and Sackler Galleries is located in the Sackler. It has nearly 60,000 volumes, about half of which are in Chinese and Japanese, and subscribes to more than 400 periodicals. Researchers may examine the more than 100,000 photographic images in the archives. About 73,000 slides are available for loan. Library hours are 10 A.M. to 5 P.M., Monday through Friday. Appointments are necessary; call 202-357-4880.

Above: Raghubir Singh (b. 1942), *Men Exercise on the Sand Bank Facing Banaras*, photograph, India, 1986. Opposite top: Shindo Susumu (b. 1952), bowl, Japan, 1992, porcelain with blue enamel glaze. Opposite bottom: Two-headed bust, Jordan, ca. 6500 B.C.E., plaster and bitumen; lent by the Department of Antiquities of Jordan.

Above: Face mask, Lele peoples, Democratic Republic of the Congo, early to mid-20th century. Opposite top: Headrest, Luba peoples, Democratic Republic of the Congo, mid to late 19th century.

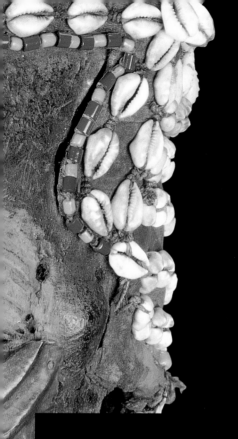

950 Independence
Avenue, SW.
Entered from Enid A.
Haupt Garden through
ground-level pavilion.
Open daily, except
December 25,
10 A.M. to 5:30 P.M.
Metrorail:
Smithsonian station.
Smithsonian
information:
202-357-2700
TTY: 202-357-4814.
www.si.edu/nmafa

# NATIONAL MUSEUM OF
# AFRICAN ART

African art represents one of humanity's
greatest achievements, fusing visual
imagery with spiritual beliefs and social
purpose. Its technical accomplishment
and artistic perfection bear witness to the
creative ingenuity of its makers. The
National Museum of African Art's collections celebrate and explore the visual arts
of the entire continent of Africa, from
ancient to contemporary times. Through
its collections, dynamic exhibitions,
imaginative educational programs, and
special collaborations with museums
worldwide, the National Museum of
African Art is raising the profile and
importance of African art

Right: Head, Edo peoples, Benin Kingdom, Nigeria, late 15th–early 16th century. Below: Crown, Yoruba peoples, Ijebu region, Nigeria, ca. 1930. Opposite top: Face mask, Chowke peoples, Democratic Republic of the Congo, early 20th century. Opposite bottom: Olowe of Ise (Nigerian, ca. 1875–ca. 1938), Yoruba peoples, *Bowl with Figures*, ca. 1925.

## EXHIBITIONS

To build in-depth understanding of cultures in which art and life are one, the National Museum of African Art's exhibitions present the finest examples of sculpture and masks, architectural elements, utilitarian objects, textiles, objects of adornment, archival photographs, and contemporary art in all media. The museum's collections are regularly rotated throughout four permanent exhibitions: "Images of Power and Identity," "Art of the Personal Object," "The Ancient West African City of Benin," and "The Ancient Nubian City of Kerma." Three changing galleries include the Sylvia H. Williams Gallery for contemporary African art, the Point of View Gallery for small, permanent-collection, focused exhibitions, and the second-level gallery. Also on the second level are a lecture hall, an educational workshop, a library, and the Eliot Elisofon Photographic Archives.

## PUBLIC PROGRAMS

More than 30 million Americans trace their heritage to the cultures and traditions of Africa. With a variety of programs and resources for people of all ages, the museum is a portal to African arts and culture. It offers guided tours, workshops, scholarly symposia, music and dance programs, films, teacher training workshops, audiovisual loan programs, and much more. "AfriKid Art" features African music, hands-on workshops, storytelling, and special tours for children of all ages. The "Images of Power and Identity Family Guide" promotes interaction between adults and children in the permanent-collection galleries. Information about public programs and exhibitions is published in the museum's quarterly calendar and is

Right: Garth Erasmus
(South African, b. 1956),
*The Muse #3*, 1995.
Below: *Untitled #1*,
Magdalene Anyango N.
Odundo (b. 1950, Nairobi,
Kenya), 1994. Opposite:
Constance Larrabee
(American, b. South
Africa, 1915–2000),
*Zulu Girl and Children*,
near Ixopo, Natal, South
Africa, 1949.

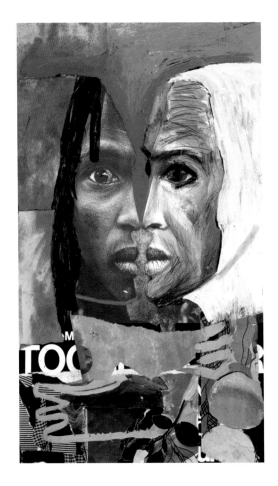

available at the museum's Web site. To receive the calendar, write to: Calendar, National Museum of African Art, Smithsonian Institution, Washington, D.C. 20560-0708.

## RESEARCH FACILITIES

The National Museum of African Art is a leading research and reference center for the arts of Africa. The Eliot Elisofon Photographic Archives, with 300,000 photographic prints and transparencies, extensive unedited film footage, and videos and documentary films on African art,

specializes in the collection and preservation of visual materials on African art, culture, and the environment. The hours are from 10 A.M. to 4 P.M., Monday through Friday, by appointment; call 202-357-4600, ext. 281. The Warren M. Robbins Library, named for the museum's founder, contains more than 28,000 volumes on African art and material culture. The library is open from 9 A.M. to 5:15 P.M., Monday through Friday, by appointment; call 202-357-4600, ext. 286.

### INFORMATION DESK

**In the entrance pavilion**

### TOURS

**Museum tours are offered for individuals on a walk-in basis. Tours for school and community groups are available by appointment. To request a tour schedule or to make an appointment, call 202-357-4600, ext. 222, or 202-357-4814 (TTY).**

### MUSEUM STORE

**African jewelry, textiles, sculpture, musical recordings, books, exhibition catalogues, posters, and postcards are for sale.**

Above: The Arts and Industries Building rotunda.

900 Jefferson Drive, SW
(next to the
Smithsonian Castle).
Open daily, except
December 25, 10 A.M.
to 5:30 P.M.
Metrorail:
Smithsonian station.
Smithsonian
information:
202-357-2700
TTY: 202-357-1729.
www.si.edu/ai

## ARTS AND INDUSTRIES BUILDING

To step into the Arts and Industries Building, located just east of the Castle, is to step back to 1881. That was the year that the building opened in time for the Inaugural Ball of President James A. Garfield. Over the years the Arts and Industries Building has served as a special venue for many popular objects and exhibitions, from the First Ladies' gowns to the *Spirit of St. Louis* to the long-running "1876: A Centennial Exhibition."

The three main halls of the Arts and Industries Building currently host a wide variety of large-scale changing exhibitions on such topics as art, history, science, and culture. The exhibitions represent the Smithsonian collections and research as well as those from other museums, galleries, universities, and archives. The North Hall features smaller changing exhibitions in addition to a café and a museum store.

View of the Arts and Industries Building from the Hirshhorn Museum and Sculpture Garden. *Last Conversation Piece*, 1994–95, by Spanish artist Juan Muñoz (1953–2001) is in the foreground.

## THE BUILDING

This exuberant Victorian structure of red brick and Ohio sandstone, with its colorful maze of roof angles, towers, and clerestories, was designed by Washingtonian architect Adolph Cluss. Completed in 1881, it is the second oldest Smithsonian building on the National Mall. Originally known as the United States National Museum, it was built to house objects given to the Institution after the Centennial Exposition closed.

Since its inception, the Arts and Industries Building, as it was eventually renamed, housed a variety of collections that have been moved to other Smithsonian museums. In 1976, its fine halls were partially restored to the Victorian style for the nation's Bicentennial celebration.

## ROTUNDA

The Rotunda features ongoing seasonal presentations of horticultural displays designed and managed by the Smithsonian's Horticulture Services Division.

## INFORMATION DESK

At the north entrance

## TOURS

Tours may be available for some exhibitions. For information call 202-357-2700, or 202-357-1729 (TTY).

## MUSEUM STORE

The museum store offers a selection of books, music, apparel, note cards, jewelry, and toys that support the changing exhibitions in the galleries.

## FOOD SERVICE

A newly added visitor amenity is a coffee kiosk serving a variety of beverages, light fare, and snacks.

## DISCOVERY THEATER

Discovery Theater, a division of The Smithsonian Associates, is located on the ground floor on the west side of the Arts and Industries Building. October through July, the theater presents live performances for children, including original productions, contemporary and traditional live puppetry, plays, dance, storytelling, and musicals—all designed to entertain, educate, and enlighten young audiences. Shows are Monday through Friday with special Saturday events scheduled. For times and reservations, call 202-357-1500 (voice and TTY).

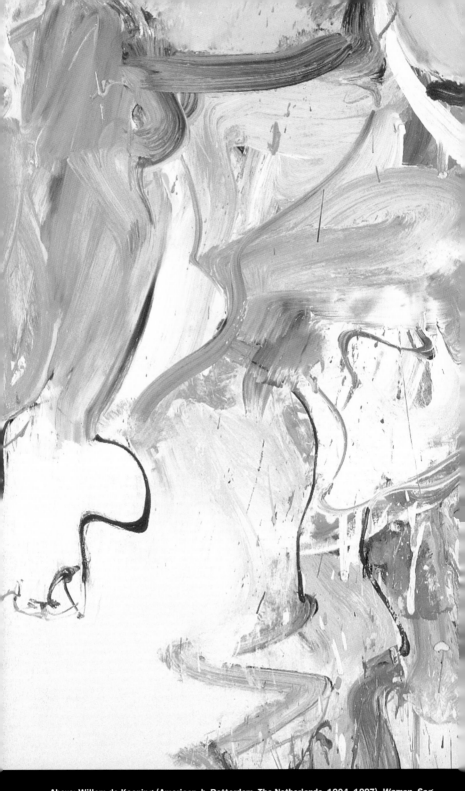

**Above: Willem de Kooning (American, b. Rotterdam, The Netherlands, 1904–1997),** *Woman, Sag Harbor* (detail), 1964. Opposite top: Claes Oldenburg (American, b. Sweden, 1929), *Z-Up*, 1961.

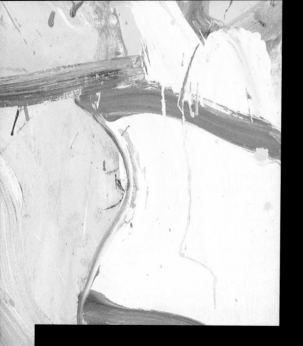

# HIRSHHORN MUSEUM AND SCULPTURE GARDEN

Independence Avenue at 7th Street, SW. Building and Plaza entered from Independence Avenue; Plaza and Sculpture Garden entered from National Mall. Open daily, except December 25: building, 10 A.M. to 5:30 P.M.; Plaza, 7:30 A.M. to 5:30 P.M.; Sculpture Garden, 7:30 A.M. to dusk. Metrorail: L'Enfant Plaza station. Smithsonian information: 202-357-2700 TTY: 202-633-8043. hirshhorn.si.edu

This strikingly designed museum of modern and contemporary art is named after the dedicated and enthusiastic American collector of art Joseph H. Hirshhorn (1899–1981). His gifts and bequest to the nation of more than 12,000 works are the nucleus of a dynamic collection that remains current through purchases and gifts from many donors. When the museum opened in 1974, the Smithsonian offered, for the first time, a capsule history of modern art in a building and sunken garden that were bold, even daring, by contemporary architectural standards.

Today, the museum is for many the most challenging and visually stimulating of the Institution's attractions on the National Mall. Museum goers may be dazzled or perplexed by what is on view, but

**Top: David Smith (American, 1906–1965), *Cubi XII*, 1963. Above: Mark di Suvero (American, b. Shanghai, 1933), *Are Years What? (for Marianne Moore)*, 1967. Right: Constantin Brancusi (Romanian, 1876–1957), *Torso of a Young Man*, 1924.**

the experience is seldom boring. Art, especially new art, can evoke powerful responses.

Works from the permanent collection on public display are rotated, so what may be seen in any of the galleries at any given time will vary. In addition, important temporary exhibitions may fill some second-floor galleries and the third-floor "Directions" gallery, which rotates one-room installations by emerging artists.

## A PLACE FOR SCULPTURE . . .

Sculpture was a special passion of the museum's founding donor, and the Hirshhorn's sculpture collection is one of the most distinguished in the world. Sculptures by international artists can be seen throughout the museum building, mixed in with the paintings or in mini-surveys along window walls overlooking the fountain, as well as amid the greenery of the outdoor fountain plaza and along pathways of the Sculpture Garden. There, adjacent to the National Mall, are several signature works: Auguste Rodin's figure ensemble of 1884–89, *Monument to the Burghers of Calais*; compositions by mid-century sculptural giants Alexander Calder, Henry Moore, and David Smith; and the definitive, soaring red steel construction by Mark di Suvero, *Are Years What? (for Marianne Moore)*, 1967, to name a few.

Closer to the museum itself, contemporary sculpture is the keynote: here, with the building hovering above, are Juan Muñoz's interacting bronze figures resembling ventriloquists' dummies, *Last Conversation Piece*, 1994–95, and Tony Smith's minimal yet intricate *Throwback*, 1976–79, among others.

## . . . AND THE ART OF OUR TIME

The diversity of styles, themes, and media pursued by an international mix of artists from the dawn of the 20th century to the present unfolds in "Celebrating Modern Art" and "Celebrating Contemporary Art." This two-part in-

**Wolfgang Laib (German, b. 1950),** *Pollen from Hazelnut,* **1998–2000.**

stallation of the permanent collection, which fills the third floor and the lower level, respectively, opens on the third floor with keenly observed scenes of American life by Edward Hopper and others. Proceeding around the circle, one encounters early modernists Stanton MacDonald Wright and Marsden Hartley adapting Cubism's faceted forms, and Fernand Léger and Constantin Brancusi paring the figure down to its essence. As the century progresses, landscapes of organic form, some tied to Surrealism, appear by Georgia O'Keeffe, Isamu Noguchi, René Magritte, and Joan Miró. Vivid, often tormented expressions in paint and bronze by Europeans Francis Bacon and Alberto Giacometti usher in the postwar years in dialogue with dynamic gestures of New York School and West Coast paintings by Willem de Kooning, Richard Diebenkorn, and others. Completing the circle are works associated with Pop Art of the 1960s by Claes Oldenburg and others, and Nam June Paik's *Video Flag,* 1985–96, a mesmerizing example of a new art form that offers a foretaste of "Celebrating

Above: Chuck Close (American, b. 1940), *Roy II*, 1994. Opposite: Georgia O'Keeffe (American, 1887–1986), *Goat's Horn with Red*, 1945.

Contemporary Art" two flights down. There, the emphasis on the "new"—newly conceived, newly created, newly acquired—distinguishes a selection of works ranging from Rachel Whiteread's *Untitled (Library)*, a sculptural installation of life-size bookshelves related to her Vienna Holocaust Memorial, to Chuck Close's gridded profile portrait of artist Roy Lichtenstein, and Andy Warhol's compelling four-face self-portrait. Works seen on the lower level change regularly. Whether revealing personal histories, world events, the media's influence, or new forms of beauty, they always resonate strongly with contemporary life.

## LOOK, LEARN, CREATE

The Hirshhorn offers a range of educational experiences for young and old alike, from formal lectures by artists and curators to an independent film series, from informative guided tours of the permanent collection to user-friendly programs, workshops, and self-guided gallery explorations that provide venues for family fun, personal revelation, and community interaction. Museum educators collaborate with teachers and students to plan tours and activities that meet curriculum goals. Families may participate in "Young at Art" workshops, where children ages 6 to 9 and their adult companions make objects and discover art

together, tour the galleries with activity sheets that conclude with creative projects in frequent "Improv Art" sessions, enjoy Family Days of performances, treasure hunts, refreshments, and yet more art activities, or explore specific works with the *Family Guide,* a free publication that takes visitors on a self-guided tour through its color-coded "art cards." The "Art Explorers" series offers adults behind-the-scenes tours and hands-on projects; "Writers Workshops" encourage the creation of poetry and prose based on art; and "Art After Hours" are nighttime fetes with tours, object making, and films. Emerging art historians speak

As the Smithsonian's showcase for modern and contemporary art, the Hirshhorn Museum and Sculpture Garden provides a comprehensive look at art from the first stirrings of modernism in the 19th century to the most recent developments in the art of our time. Sculpture by modern masters (much of it situated outdoors), international modernist works of the postwar era, and contemporary art are particular attractions. American and European variations on Cubism, Social Realism, Surrealism, Geometric Abstraction, and Expressionism trace modern art past the mid-20th century. Contemporary currents range from Pop Art of the 1960s to recent explorations by emerging artists working in a variety of media.

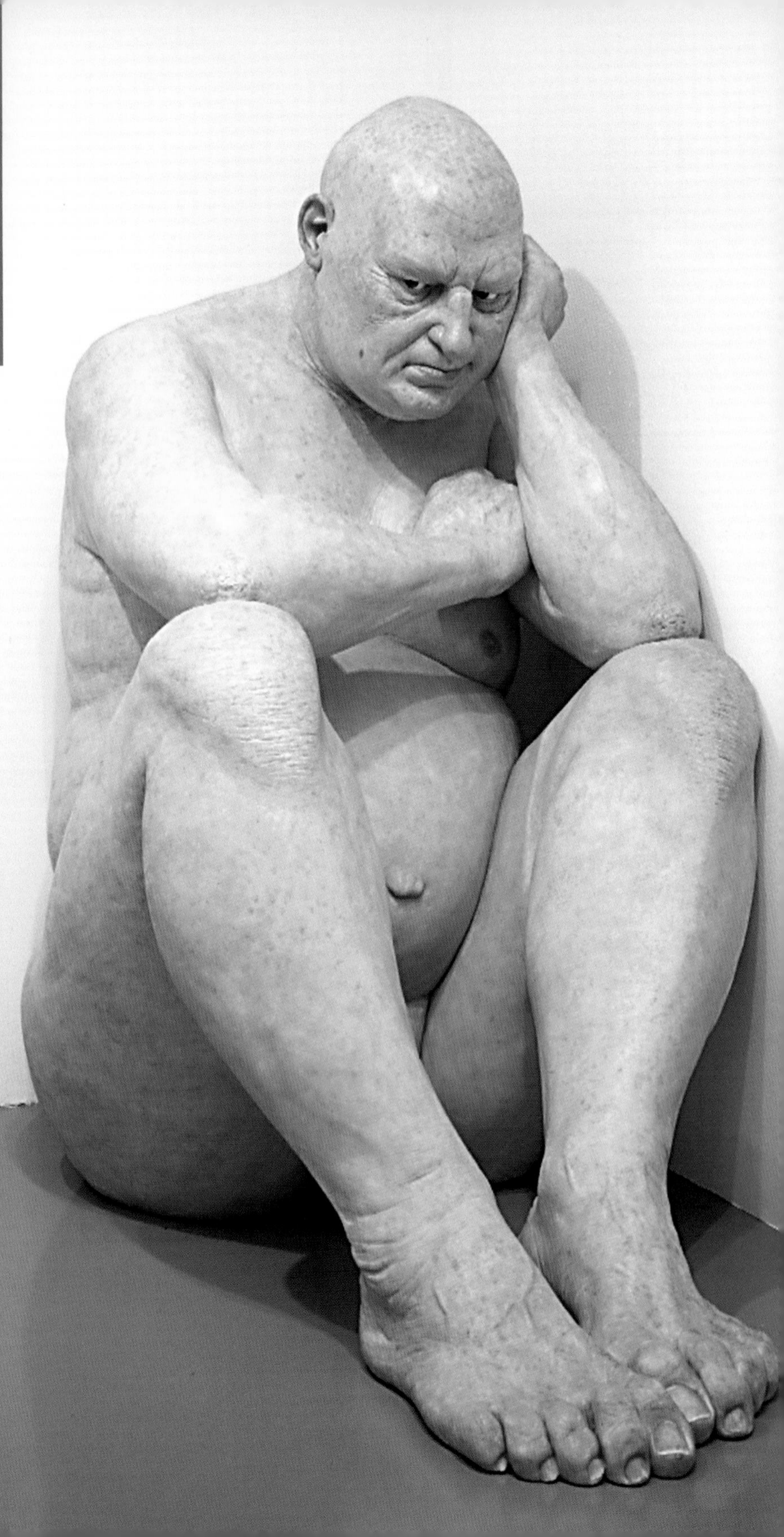

at the "New Voices" exhibition tours; monthly "First Friday" talks hone in on single artworks; and the "Meet the Artist" series brings visitors to the crux of the matter: artists exhibiting works in museum exhibitions explain their motivations and sources.

## A BOLD SETTING

Gordon Bunshaft (1909–1990), winner in 1987 of the Pritzker Prize in architecture, designed the Hirshhorn complex. Redesigns of the Sculpture Garden in 1981 and the Plaza in 1993 increased accessibility and enhanced the placement of sculpture with additional greenery. The dynamic and unorthodox building—82 feet high and 231 feet in diameter—encircles an open courtyard and an asymmetrically placed bronze fountain. The exterior wall is a solid surface, broken only by a window 70 feet long in the third-floor Abram Lerner Room, from which visitors may enjoy a spectacular view of the National Mall. Floor-to-ceiling windows define the inner core, which overlooks the fountain. Four massive piers elevate the concrete structure above the walled plaza. The recessed garden across Jefferson Drive, with its rectangular reflecting pool, provides a peaceful area for viewing art.

**Above: Dana Hoey (American, b. 1966), *Waimea*, 2000. Opposite: Ron Mueck (Australian, b. 1958), *Untitled (Big Man)*, 2000.**

Above: Andy Warhol
(American, 1928–1987),
*Self-Portrait*, 1986.
© The Andy Warhol Foun-
dation for the Visual
Arts / ARS, New York.
Right: Stephan Balkenhol
(German, b. 1957), *Three
Hybrids*, 1995. Opposite
top: Richard Diebenkorn
(American, 1922–1993),
*Man and Woman in a
Large Room*, 1957.
Opposite bottom:
Robert Gober (American,
b. 1954), *Untitled*, 1990.

Outdoors at the Hirshhorn, benches, shaded areas,
and fountainside tables at a summertime café provide
attractive spots in which to linger and snack. Please
enjoy—but do not touch the sculptures!

Located in the lobby and staffed until 4 P.M. daily. Exhibitions and events are posted here.

## TOURS

Docent-led tours of the permanent collection are offered Monday through Friday at 10:30 A.M. and 12 noon, and Saturday and Sunday at 12 noon and

2 P.M. Tours for groups with up to 90 participants can be scheduled with three weeks' advance notice. Tours of the Sculpture Garden are available May through October and other times upon request, weather permitting. Times of the tours vary. The Education Department offers tours in French, Spanish, German, Russian, and Thai upon request. Sign-language tours and "Touch Tours" of the sculpture collection for visitors who are blind or have limited vision are also available; contact the department for further information. Call 202-357-3235, ext. 117, or 202-633-8043 (TTY).

## PUBLIC PROGRAMS

A variety of free films, lectures, symposia, and talks by artists are presented regularly in the Marion and Gustave Ring Auditorium on the lower level. Other programs include gallery talks, workshops for a variety of audiences, "drop-in" family art activities, summer music concerts, and outreach programs for teachers, schools, and community groups. For information, call 202-357-2700, or 202-633-8043 (TTY).

## CAFÉ

Full Circle, an outdoor, self-service, luncheon café on the museum's plaza, is open daily from late May through Labor Day weekend.

## MUSEUM STORE

Located on the plaza level, the museum store offers exhibition catalogues, slides, postcards, reproductions, books on art, and other items related to the museum's programs.

**Above: M. F. K. Fisher (1908–1992) by Ginny Stanford, acrylic on canvas (detail), 1991.**

**© Ginny Stanford. Opposite top: Rosa Parks (b. 1913) by Marshall D. Rumbaugh,**

**limewood, 1983.**

8th and F Streets, NW.
Temporarily closed
for renovation.
Metrorail:
Gallery Place station.
Museum information:
202-275-1738.
Smithsonian
information:
202-357-2700
TTY: 202-357-1729.
www.npg.si.edu

# NATIONAL PORTRAIT GALLERY

The American nation has set aside a place
to keep generations of remarkable Americans in the company of their fellow citizens: the National Portrait Gallery. It is
the place where the arts tell the stories of
lives lived across centuries of our experience as a society, one that continually
reinvents itself and tests its ideals.
Through the visual, performing, literary,
and electronic arts, the National Portrait
Gallery provides a stage for George
Washington and Martin Luther King, for
Marilyn Monroe and Babe Ruth, among
thousands of others, to share with us who
they were and what they mean to us.

The National Portrait Gallery currently
exists everywhere but in the magnificent
building it normally inhabits. Closed for
renovation in 2000, the Patent Office
Building is undergoing extensive work

Below: Robert F. Kennedy (1925–1968) by Roy Lichtenstein, lithograph on paper, 1989. Gift of *Time* magazine. © Estate of Roy Lichtenstein. Opposite: George Washington (1732–1799), "Lansdowne" portrait by Gilbert Stuart, oil on canvas, 1796. Acquired as a gift to the nation through the generosity of the Donald W. Reynolds Foundation.

to recall the elegance of its origins in the 19th century (beginning in 1836) and to welcome the technologies of the 21st century. The third oldest public building in the city, after the White House and the Capitol, and praised by Walt Whitman as "the noblest of Washington buildings," it was saved from the wrecking ball in 1958 and then welcomed the opening of the National Portrait Gallery in 1968. That was no accident. Pierre L'Enfant, in his design for the new federal city, had envisioned for this site a place to honor the nation's heroes. In our own time, a building is being reborn and a vision fulfilled.

While the building may be temporarily closed, the museum is certainly not. Visitors to Washington, D.C., will find that the Portrait Gallery has teamed with other museums and venues in the area to present performances that capture the lives of entertaining Americans: "Portrait Stories," storytelling to children about inspiring lives; lectures about poets and politicians; and exhibitions about fascinating people. Consult lists of the city's attractions to find the performances.

For those who cannot come to Washington, the National Portrait Gallery will come to them. Under the banner of our "Portrait of the Nation" initiative, the Gallery is traveling paintings, photographs, drawings, and caricatures of the great and the near-great that would normally remain within the walls of the museum. Our "museum without walls" can be visited at sites throughout the country in "Portraits of the Presidents," which represents a national collection of presidential portraits comparable to that of the White House; "A Brush with History," which includes some of the most compelling portraits of Americans from Benjamin Franklin to Sequoya to Lena Horne; and "Eye Contact," which celebrates the intimacy of the portrait drawing.

Many communities in America will also enjoy the
historic opportunity to see what may rightly be
called the most powerful portrait in American history, the full-length "Lansdowne" portrait of our first
President, George Washington, painted in 1796 by

**Marilyn Monroe (1926–1962) by David D. Geary, color positive transparency, 1954. Gift of the artist.**

the greatest portraitist of his era, Gilbert Stuart. This is the George Washington America needed to believe in when it was an untried new nation. On 33-year loan to the National Portrait Gallery, where it has held pride of place, the painting that has captured the imagination of many generations was at risk of being sold at auction by its English owner. A national appeal in 2001 led to its being saved for the nation by the Donald W. Reynolds Foundation of Las Vegas, Nevada. The generosity of that foundation has also led to the support of a national tour of this American icon until the Portrait Gallery reopens. George Washington will "visit" parts of the nation that did not exist in his lifetime but represent the full benefit of his enduring legacy.

The electronic National Portrait Gallery provides another way to meet extraordinary Americans through the paintings, sculpture, photographs, prints, and drawings represented in the museum's collections and exhibitions. Our Web site, one of the most popular among Smithsonian museums, allows the electronic visitor to experience a virtual visit to our Hall of Presidents and to 20 of our past exhibitions. Visitors will also be able to search for records of portraits in the collection of the National Portrait Gallery—which now boasts more than 18,000 objects—and those identified in other collections by our Catalog of American Portraits. The museum's plans for the future include the creation of exhibitions specifically for the electronic audience. An example, which can now be viewed at www.civilwar.si.edu, is "Civil War@Smithsonian," produced by the National Portrait Gallery and dedicated to examining the war through the Smithsonian's extensive collections. Many of the objects presented on the site have not been exhibited in recent times. Of special

**Charlie Chaplin (1889–1977) by Edward Steichen, gelatin silver print, 1925. Acquired in memory of Agnes and Eugene Meyer through the generosity of Katharine Graham and the New York Community Trust, The Island Fund. © Joanna T. Steichen.**

## AT A GLANCE

Through the visual, performing, literary, and electronic arts, the National Portrait Gallery provides a stage for remarkable Americans to share with us who they were and what they mean to us. Objects from the Gallery's collections are currently on tour. Presentations include Gilbert Stuart's "Lansdowne" painting of George Washington, perhaps the most powerful portrait in America's history, as well as exhibitions on the presidents, paintings, photographs, and drawings. In addition to its popular Web site, the Gallery has produced "Civil War@Smithsonian" highlighting the Smithsonian's Civil War collections.

**John Brown (1800–1859) by Augustus Washington, daguerreotype, ca. 1846/47. Purchased with major acquisition funds and with funds donated by Betty Adler Schermer in honor of her great-grandfather, August M. Bondi.**

interest will be objects that relate to slavery and the Emancipation Proclamation, the army and navy, the home front, and the Smithsonian itself.

The Portrait Gallery has not, of course, abandoned the printed page, and takes pride in the many books associated with its exhibitions. Beginning with the summer of 2000, the museum has published a quarterly newsletter, *Profile*, in a magazine

format. Recent issues have been devoted to the topic of biography and biographers as well as to the extraordinary women represented in the Portrait Gallery's collection and to the presidency as an ongoing national fascination.

The museum is also a resource center for biography and portraiture, offering research services through several offices by appointment. Extensive biographical files are kept in the Office of the Historian. The Catalog of American Portraits, a unique national reference center, contains documentation, including photographs, for nearly 200,000 portraits of

Arnold Palmer (b. 1929) by Paul Burns, oil on canvas, 1979. Gift of the family of Paul C. Burns.

noted Americans, located in public and private collections throughout the country. The library, shared with the Smithsonian American Art Museum, contains 150,000 volumes, receives more than 1,000 periodicals, offers selected electronic resources, and has an extensive collection of clippings and pamphlets on art subjects. The Peale Family Papers, devoted to research on the work and lives of this prominent Philadelphia family of artists and naturalists, provides information and materials relating to American cultural and social development from the mid-18th to the late 19th century.

8th and G Streets, NW.
Temporarily closed
for renovation.
Metrorail:
Gallery Place station.
Museum information:
202-275-1500.
Smithsonian
information:
202-357-2700.
Recorded information:
202-633-8998
TTY: 202-357-4522.
AmericanArt.si.edu

# SMITHSONIAN

# AMERICAN

# ART MUSEUM

The Smithsonian American Art Museum is dedicated to the art and artists of the United States. All regions, cultures, and traditions in this country are represented in the museum's collections, research resources, exhibitions, and public programs.

The museum began in 1829 with gifts from private collections and art organizations. It has grown steadily to become a center for the study, enjoyment, and preservation of America's visual arts. Today, the collection is the world's most important American art holdings with approximately 39,000 artworks in all media, spanning more than 300 years of artistic achievement.

While undergoing renovation, the museum is coordinating the nation's most extensive art tour ever, *Treasures to Go.* Comprising eight traveling exhibitions

**Abbott Handerson Thayer (1849–1921),** *Angel,* **1887.**

thanks to the support of the Principal Financial Group.® The museum also continues to offer an array of activities, information, and images on its award-winning Web site, AmericanArt.si.edu.

As a major center for research in American art, the museum includes such resources as the Inventory of American Paintings Executed before 1914, with data on nearly 270,000 works; the Peter A. Juley & Sons collection of 127,000 historic photographs; the Slide and Photographic Archives; the Pre-1877 Art Exhibition

Catalogue Index; the Inventory of American Sculpture, with information on more than 80,000 indoor and outdoor works; and the Joseph Cornell Study Center.

## HISTORY

The Smithsonian American Art Museum, the oldest national art collection in the United States, predates the founding of the Smithsonian Institution. Praised by Walt Whitman as "the noblest of Washington buildings," the museum's historic home, the Old Patent

Office, is considered the finest example of Greek Revival architecture in the United States. Begun in 1836 and completed in 1867, the building was the third major federal building constructed in Washington.

    Clara Barton tended wounded Union soldiers in the building when it served as a hospital and temporary barracks during the Civil War. In March 1865, it was the site of Abraham Lincoln's second inaugural ball. During its use as a patent office, inventors including Alexander Graham Bell and Thomas Edison obtained

**Albert Pinkham Ryder (1847–1917),** *Flying Dutchman,* **1887.**

Above: John Singer Sargent (1856–1925), *Elizabeth Winthrop Chanler*, 1893. Opposite: George Catlin (1796–1872), *Buffalo Bull's Back Fat, head chief, Blood Tribe*, 1832.

patents for their work.

A National Historic Landmark, the Old Patent Office was saved from the wrecking ball in 1958, and Congress gave it to the Smithsonian in 1962. After extensive interior renovations to the historic structure, the museum opened to the public there in 1968. Although the museum's history spans 175 years, its collection lacked proper exhibition space until that time. In October 2000, it was renamed the Smithsonian American Art Museum to emphasize its Smithsonian association. The current renovation will restore the original grandeur of this majestic building, with new galleries in which to showcase American art.

## COLLECTIONS

The Smithsonian American Art Museum's collection tells the story of America through the visual arts. Colonial portraiture, 19th-century landscape, American Impressionism, 20th-century realism and abstraction, New Deal projects, sculpture, photography, prints and drawings, African American art, Latino art, and folk art are featured in the collection. Contemporary American crafts are featured at the Smithsonian American Art Museum's Renwick Gallery (see p. 169).

Two early Puerto Rican wood sculptures, *Santa Barbara* from about 1680 to 1690 and *Nuestra Señora de los Dolores (Our Lady of Sorrows)* from about 1675 to 1725, are the oldest works in the collection. Colonial America is represented with portraits by John Singleton Copley, Charles Willson Peale, and Gilbert Stuart, landscapes by Thomas Cole, and sculptures by Horatio Greenough.

For decades, the museum championed the artists who captured the spirit of the frontier and the lure of the West. George Catlin, Frederic Remington, Thomas Moran, and Albert Bierstadt celebrated the landscape and paid tribute to Native Americans and their cultures.

The museum has one of the finest and largest collections of American Impressionist paintings and artwork from the last quarter of the 19th century, a period dubbed the "Gilded Age" by author Mark Twain. Artists included are Childe Hassam, Mary Cassatt, William Merritt Chase, Winslow Homer, John Singer Sargent, and James McNeill Whistler.

The country's largest collection of New Deal art and murals can also

**Above: David Hockney (b. 1937), *Double Entrance*, 1993–95.**
**Below: Nam June Paik (b. 1932), *Technology*, 1991.**

be found at the Smithsonian American Art Museum. Realist painters include Edward Hopper, John Sloan, and Andrew Wyeth.

Some American modernists, like Georgia O'Keeffe and Joseph Stella, captured the spirit of their age with inventive new ways of depicting the world, while artists such as Willem de Kooning and Franz Kline created wholly abstract compositions. Other important 20th-century painters in the collection are Marsden Hartley, Stuart Davis, Wayne Thiebaud, Alfred Jensen, and Philip Guston.

In recent years, the museum has strengthened its commitment to contemporary artists through a number of important acquisitions, including works by Jennifer Bartlett, Chuck Close, Eric Fischl, Nam June Paik, Renee Stout, and Mark Tansey.

The museum's sculpture collection, ranging from works by 19th-century masters Horatio Greenough, Edmonia Lewis, Harriet Hosmer, and Augustus Saint-Gaudens to renowned 20th-century artists Louise Nevelson, Isamu Noguchi, and Edward Kienholz, is the largest collection of American sculpture anywhere. Works on paper

comprise a large part of the collection, notably prints from the 20th century and more than 150 years of photography.

William H. Johnson (1901–1970), *Early Morning Work*, about 1940.

The Smithsonian American Art Museum also has a long tradition of championing works that initially did not have a place in the story of American art. The museum was one of the first museums to collect and display folk art in its galleries. In the last decade, it has acquired almost 500 pieces of Latino art, spanning colonial times to today.

Extensive holdings by William H. Johnson are part of the museum's notable collection of more than 2,000 artworks by African American artists. Other African American artists represented include Robert Scott Duncanson, Henry Ossawa Tanner, Horace Pippin, Romare Bearden, Jacob Lawrence, Louis Mailou Jones, and Sam Gilliam.

# RENWICK GALLERY OF THE SMITHSONIAN AMERICAN ART MUSEUM

Pennsylvania Avenue at 17th Street, NW (one block west of the White House). Open daily, except December 25, 10 A.M. to 5:30 P.M. Metrorail: Farragut West station (17th Street exit). Museum information: 202-275-1500. Smithsonian information: 202-357-2700. Recorded information: 202-633-8998 TTY: 202-357-4522. AmericanArt.si.edu

The Renwick Gallery, a curatorial department of the Smithsonian American Art Museum, exhibits the creative work of American craft artists. Built during the Civil War period, the building that now houses the Renwick Gallery was the city's first art museum—the original Corcoran Gallery of Art. In 1965, when the building was threatened with demolition, it was transferred to the Smithsonian Institution, extensively renovated, and renamed for its architect, James Renwick.

Today, the museum collects the work of artists who are important in the development of 20th- and 21st-century American crafts. Changing exhibitions from the permanent collection of some 2,000 objects of glass, metal, ceramics, wood, and fiber are shown on the second floor. The many artists represented include Anni Albers, Wendell Castle, Dale Chihuly,

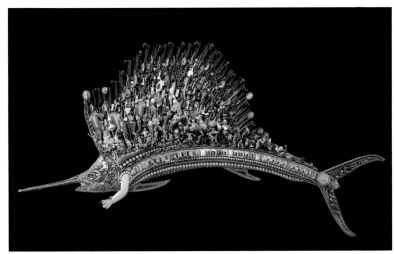

Changing exhibitions of American crafts and decorative arts—historic and contemporary as well as selections from the permanent collection of 20th- and 21st-century American crafts—are on view in this distinguished building. The Grand Salon is elegantly furnished in the opulent style of the 1860s and 1870s.

William Harper, Larry Fuente, Harvey Littleton, Albert Paley, Peter Voulkos, and Betty Woodman.

The special exhibition program addresses major issues in American crafts and decorative arts, including sources, influences, and earlier historical traditions. Recent special exhibitions include those on loan, such as "Spirits of the Cloth: Contemporary Quilts by African American artists," permanent-collection exhibitions focusing on the five craft media such as "USA Clay," and major retrospectives such as "The Furniture of Sam Maloof."

## THE BUILDING

The building itself is a major artistic achievement. Its restoration is in part a result of the effort to preserve the character of the Lafayette Park–Pennsylvania Avenue area near the White House. This handsome structure is a notable example of French Second

Empire style. William Wilson Corcoran's monogram and profile portrait appear with the motto "Dedicated to Art" over the front entrance.

Construction began in 1858, but the Civil War intervened; from 1861 to 1869, the building was a warehouse for military materiel and the headquarters of the quartermaster general. Although the interior was not completed until 1874, a gala public preview was held in February 1871 with President and Mrs. Ulysses S. Grant presiding over a grand ball to raise additional funds for the Washington Monument.

**Above: Galleries display crafts from the permanent collection. Photo © Robert Lautman. Opposite top: Larry Fuente (b. 1947), *Game Fish*, 1988. © 1988 Larry Fuente. Opposite bottom: Jon Eric Riis (b. 1945), *Pair of Prickly Pears*, 1997.**

Above: Harvey Littleton (b. 1922), *Opalescent Red Crown*, 1983. Opposite: The Grand Salon of the Renwick Gallery provides a beautiful Victorian space for the display of the collection. Photo © Robert Lautman.

Corcoran's collections occupied the building from 1874 until 1897, when they were moved to the new Corcoran Gallery of Art, three blocks south on 17th Street and New York Avenue. The U.S. Court of Claims used the building for 65 years beginning in 1899.

The Grand Salon, exemplifying the splendor of a sumptuous Victorian salon of the 1860s and 1870s, is one of the most spectacular spaces in Washington. Refurbished in 2000, the room boasts custom-made draperies and 40-foot ceilings with gilded frieze elements among the components that re-create the elegant setting of a 19th-century collector's picture gallery. Among the 170 artworks on view from the Smithsonian American Art Museum, currently closed for renovation, are three monumental paintings of Yellowstone and the Grand Canyon by Thomas Moran, two on long-term loan from the U.S. Department of the Interior.

INFORMATION DESK

**At the entrance**

## TOURS

Group tours for students and adults may be arranged in advance. For reservations, call 202-633-8070, or 202-357-4522 (TTY). Sign language and oral interpreters are available on request for tours and public programs with one week's notice.

## PUBLIC PROGRAMS

Free public programs include craft demonstrations, gallery talks, films, and illustrated lectures. For information,

call 202-357-2700, or 202-357-4522 (TTY), or visit the Web site AmericanArt.si.edu.

## MUSEUM STORE

The museum store features Renwick publications and other craft and decorative art books, craft objects relating to exhibitions, postcards, note cards, holiday cards, posters, calendars, and jewelry.

Above: Sorting mail on moving trains, which began after the Civil War, was one of the postal service's great innovations. Opposite top: This badge was worn by a pilot in the Airmail Service, in operation from August 12, 1918, to September 1, 1927, during which time more than 6,500 planes were forced to land and 32 pilots died flying.

2 Massachusetts
Avenue at First
Street, NE
(in the Washington
City Post Office
Building next to
Union Station).
Open daily, except
December 25,
10 A.M. to 5:30 P.M.
Metrorail:
Union Station.
Information:
202-357-2991
TTY: 202-633-9849.
www.si.edu/postal

# NATIONAL POSTAL MUSEUM

We are a migratory people. Our brothers, our neighbors, our children go away from us and the means of communication with them by letter and newspapers is one of the strongest ties that binds [*sic*] us together.

*Congressman Horace Maynard,*
*Tennessee, 1859*

Mail touches everyone, making the boundaries of postal history limitless. America's postal history can be defined through the use of objects as small as stamps and as mammoth as airplanes. It is expressed in heartrending letters from soldiers on foreign battlefields and through the explosion of direct-mail marketing. America's postal service was the force behind the creation of commercial aviation. It helped push the development of cross-country stagecoach routes

and railroads. It ensured the development and perpetual maintenance of rural roads. The postal service was where thousands of African Americans were first able to obtain government employment. America's postal history is the story of the people who made the service work and those who used it. It is the history of mail and the American people.

The National Postal Museum opened on July 30, 1993. Located on Capitol Hill, the museum is housed in

the Old City Post Office Building. The building, designed by Daniel Burnham, was built between 1911 and 1914. It is a classic Beaux Arts–style structure that complements its next-door neighbor, the Burnham-designed Union Station. The museum has 23,000 square feet of exhibition space, a research library, a stamp store, and a museum store.

The ornate historic lobby formerly served as the main service area of the City Post Office Building. By the 1970s that part of the building had been modernized to an unrecognizable point, a hodge-podge of Formica™ and harsh fluorescent lighting. Painstaking renovation begun in 1989 restored every foot of the lobby to its original glamour. Today, the lobby is the foyer to the National Postal Museum.

## BINDING THE NATION

This gallery traces events from colonial times through the 19th century, stressing the importance of written communication in the development of the new nation.

As early as 1673, regular mail was carried between New York and Boston following Indian trails. As co-deputy postmaster for the colonies, Benjamin Franklin played a key role in establishing mail service. After the Revolution, Americans recognized that the postal service, and the news and information it carried, was essential to binding the nation together. By 1800, mail was carried over more than 9,000 miles of postal roads. The challenge of developing mail service over long distances is the central theme of "The Expanding Nation," which chronicles the creation of the Butterfield Overland Mail stagecoach line and the famed Pony Express. An interactive video station invites visitors to create their own postal routes.

**Above: Children especially enjoy climbing aboard a replica of a 19th-century mudwagon, a Western-style stagecoach. Opposite: Revenue stamps were first issued in 1862 and continued after the war. In the early 1870s, they ranged in denomination from one cent to $5,000, like this example, which was approved but never issued.**

Above: Concord coaches, such as this one from 1851, could hold up to twelve passengers and the mail. Opposite top: This handstamp was salvaged from the U.S.S. *Oklahoma*, which sank at Pearl Harbor in 1941. Opposite bottom: Eddie Gardner wore this helmet when flying for the Airmail Service in 1918 as protection in the open cockpits.

## CUSTOMERS AND COMMUNITIES

By the turn of the 20th century the nation's population was expanding, as was mail volume and the need for personal mail delivery. Crowded cities and the requirements of rural Americans inspired the invention of new delivery methods. Facets of the developing system and its important role in the fabric of the nation are explored using photographs, mail vehicles, a variety of rural mailboxes, and other artifacts.

Parcel Post Service helped usher in an era of consumerism by the early 20th century that foreshadowed the massive mechanization and automation of mail and the mail-order industry. Today, mail service is a vital conduit for business. In the "What's in the Mail for You?" gallery, visitors can create graphic profiles of themselves as a target market for direct mailers.

## MOVING THE MAIL

Faced with the challenge of moving the mail quickly, the postal service was constantly on the lookout for the fastest transportation system available, from post riders to stagecoaches, automobiles and trucks, to trains and airplanes. These various means of transportation are the focus of the museum's atrium gallery.

After the Civil War, postal officials began to take advantage of trains for moving and sorting the mail. Railway mail clerks worked the mail while it was being carried between towns. In 1918, Airmail service was established on a regular basis between New York, Philadelphia, and Washington, D.C. Airmail contracts provided funding for the development of the commercial aviation industry.

## THE ART OF CARDS AND LETTERS

Personal letters are vivid windows into history. A series of changing exhibits in this gallery conveys the stories of families and friends who are bound together by letters over distance and across time. A poignant video is the highlight of "Mail Call," an exhibit celebrating the bond of mail between soldiers and their loved ones back home.

## ARTISTIC LICENSE:
## THE DUCK STAMP STORY

The history of Migratory Hunting stamps, commonly known as Federal Duck Stamps, is featured in the Jeanette Cantrell Rudy gallery. Funds from the sale of duck stamps have helped preserve wetland habitats since the mid-1930s. Hunters purchase the stamp for the right to

hunt waterfowl. The stamps are also popular with stamp collectors, conservationists, and art lovers.

## STAMPS AND STORIES

Since Great Britain issued the first adhesive postal stamp in 1840, stamps of every subject, shape, and design have been produced for consumer use or as collectibles. Stamps not only serve as proof of postage. They are also miniature works of art, keepsakes, rare treasures, and the workhorses of the automated postal system. Some stamps tell stories, while others contain secrets and hidden meanings.

More than 55,000 stamps from the United States and around the world are on display in the museum's pull-out frames. Using stamps from the museum's vast collection as well as fabulous items from private collections, the gallery's "Rarities Vault" features two new exhibits each year. Changing philatelic exhibits have featured Franklin D. Roosevelt's stamp sketches, the first U.S. stamps, and the 24-cent inverted Jenny airmail stamp of 1918, possibly the most famous U.S. stamp.

**Above: Stamps and other philatelic materials form the core of the museum's collections. Opposite: The Post Office Department promoted its speedy new service with posters in post offices across the country.**

public programs and events. Call 202-357-2991 to confirm hours of operation.

### PUBLIC PROGRAMS

Museum programs include postal history and philatelic lectures, panel discussions, performances, and family activities.

### RESEARCH FACILITIES

With more than 40,000 volumes and manuscripts, the museum's library is among the world's largest facilities for postal history and philatelic research. The library features a specimen study room, an audiovisual viewing room, and a rare book collection. Open by appointment, Monday through Friday from 10 A.M. to 4 P.M.; call 202-633-9370 to schedule a visit.

### MUSEUM STORE

Located near the escalators at the museum entrance, the museum store offers posters, T-shirts, stationery, postcards, pins, first-day covers, stamp-collector kits, stamp- and postal-related souvenirs, books for all ages on postal-history subjects and letter collections, and a selection of philatelic publications.

### STAMP STORE

Operated by the U.S. Postal Service, the stamp store is located opposite the museum store. Visitors may purchase a variety of current stamps and other commemorative stamp items.

### U.S. POST OFFICE

Accessible from the main hall of the museum

### ENTRANCE

Enter the lobby of the building and proceed by escalator to the floor level of the museum's 90-foot-high atrium.

### INFORMATION DESK

Off the lobby

### TOURS

One-hour museum tours originating at the information desk are offered daily at 11 A.M. and 1 P.M. Guided tours for adult and student groups may be arranged three weeks in advance. Sign language and oral interpreters for programs and tours require two weeks' advance notice.

### DISCOVERY CENTER

This education and activity room offers families an opportunity to work together on hands-on activities related to themes of the galleries. It is also a setting for

Above: Quilt, silk with embroidery, by Kissie Gray, Saudi River, South Carolina, ca. 1855.

Opposite: Anacostia Museum and Center for African American History and Culture after completion of a major renovation in 2001.

1901 Fort Place, SE.
Open daily, except
December 25,
10 A.M. to 5 P.M.
Metrorail:
Anacostia station.
Smithsonian
information:
202-357-2700
TTY: 202-357-1729.
www.si.edu/anacostia

# ANACOSTIA MUSEUM AND CENTER FOR AFRICAN AMERICAN HISTORY AND CULTURE

The Anacostia Museum and Center for African American History and Culture is devoted to increasing public understanding and awareness of the historical experiences and cultural expressions of people of African descent and heritage living in the Americas. Additionally, the museum has emerged as an innovator in developing exhibits and programs that focus on contemporary social and cultural issues.

A recent major renovation of the building has enhanced the museum's exhibition and programming spaces and expanded its library and collections-care facilities. The improvements will allow the museum to broaden its efforts to preserve and protect art, artifacts, and objects that reflect the diversity of the

The Anacostia Museum was established in 1967 as the nation's first federally funded neighborhood museum. The Anacostia Museum and Center for African American History and Culture has become a significant national and community-based cultural resource. Research, exhibition, and education activities focus on the historical experiences and cultural expressions of people of African descent and heritage living in the Americas.

**Right: This airplane, in the museum's permanent collection, was constructed by folk artist Leslie Payne as part of an installation replete with an airfield and runway, an air tower, and a machine shop. Opposite: The "Speak to My Heart" exhibition, presented at the Arts and Industries Building, explored the impact of religion and spirituality in African American daily life.**

A revolving exhibition program includes collaborative efforts with the community such as the recent exhibition "Speak to My Heart: Communities of Faith and Contemporary African American Life." An active community gallery program will give local residents a venue for exhibitions of local history and work by area artists. The museum also presents exhibitions in the Arts and Industries Building on the National Mall.

Scholars and researchers find unique opportunities to study African American history and culture at the Anacostia Museum. The museum's collections of archival materials, photographs, books, and artifacts reflect neighborhood and city history, women's history,

literature, and contemporary community life. Community-based documentation and education efforts sponsored by the museum include the Anacostia Museum Family History Group and the Collectors Group.

Research, collection development, and outreach at the museum are models for replication by other community-based museums. An active publications program features brochures, educational materials, and exhibition-related publications.

The Anacostia Museum is located in a park setting in southeast Washington, D.C., with ample parking for cars and buses. Picnic tables are located on site.

*By Metrorail and Metrobus:* Take the Green Line to the Anacostia station and transfer to the W-1 or W-2 Metrobus to the museum. *By car:* From downtown, take the Southeast Freeway (I-395) to the 11th Street Bridge and exit at Martin Luther King Jr. Avenue. At the fourth traffic light, turn left at Morris Road and drive up the hill to the museum. *From I-295 south:* Take the Howard Road exit and turn left on Howard Road. Travel to Martin Luther King Jr. Avenue and turn left. Turn right at Morris Road and continue up the hill to the museum.

On the first floor

Special activities for adults and children include lectures, workshops, films, and performances. A calendar of events is available on request. For information about exhibitions and programs, call 202-287-3369, or 202-357-1729 (TTY). To schedule a tour, call the Education Department at 202-287-3369.

The museum's Research Department provides fellowship and internship opportunities to undergraduate and graduate students in African American studies. Internships are also available in the Design and Production, Education, and Public Programs departments. Write to the Intern Coordinator, Anacostia Museum, 1901 Fort Place, SE, Washington, D.C. 20020, or call 202-287-3307.

The museum store features books, posters, compact discs, and other items related to African American culture and heritage.

Above: Tian Tian, the Zoo's male giant panda, rests in his newly renovated habitat.

Opposite top: The National Zoo is working to save the Bali mynah from extinction.

Opposite bottom: The Zoo's main pedestrian entrance is located on Connecticut Avenue.

# NATIONAL ZOOLOGICAL PARK

Entrances: Connecticut Avenue, NW (3001 block between Cathedral Avenue and Devonshire Place); Harvard Street and Adams Mill Road intersection; Beach Drive in Rock Creek Park. Open daily, except December 25. See page 197 for hours. Metrorail: Woodley Park/Zoo/ Adams Morgan station. Recorded information: 202-673-4800. Information Desk: 202-673-4717 TTY: 202-357-1729. National Zoo: www.si.edu/natzoo. Conservation and Research Center: www.si.edu/crc. FONZ: www.fonz.org

The National Zoo is known internationally for the display, breeding, and study of wild animals. Most of the Zoo's animals live in naturalistic settings that comfortably house social groups resembling those found in the wild.

Vertebrate species, representing the most spectacular and familiar forms of land animals, make up the most visible part of the collection, but invertebrate and aquatic species provide a more comprehensive picture of animal life. Educational graphics, learning carts, and family-oriented learning labs (including "How Do You Zoo?" in the Visitors Center and the Bird Resource Center in the Bird House) supplement public understanding of the park's animals and plants.

Native and ornamental plants grow throughout the 163-acre park. The Native

American Heritage Garden, African American Heritage Garden, and butterfly garden (featuring plants that attract butterflies) provide living examples of the interaction among plants, animals, and humans. Olmsted Walk, the central path, connects the major animal exhibits. It is named for the father of landscape architecture, Frederick Law Olmsted, who created the original design for the National Zoo as well as the U.S. Capitol grounds, the Washington National Cathedral grounds, and New York's Central Park.

## EXHIBITS

The giant pandas, Mei Xiang and Tian Tian, occupy the top spot on the Zoo's "must see" list. The pair's arrival in December 2000 on a 10-year loan from China marked the continuation of a long-term effort on the part of the Smithsonian Institution to cooperate with China to conserve giant pandas both in zoos and in the wild. The Panda House, renovated for the new panda pair, will serve as a model for future projects at the National Zoo.

The approach to the Bird House leads visitors over Wetlands, a series of five sheltered ponds surrounded

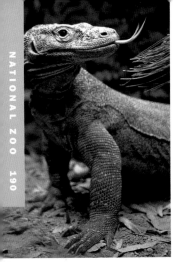

Top: The world's largest lizard, the Komodo dragon, uses its tongue to explore its environment. Bottom: The brilliantly colored green tree pythons are a favorite in the Zoo's Reptile Discovery Center.

by tall grasses, and other vegetation. The exhibit showcases the diverse but little understood wetland ecosystem and the waterfowl and wading birds native to swampy areas. The Bird House, built in 1928, includes one of the zoo world's first great flight rooms, an indoor courtyard open to both birds and visitors. Exotic, jewel-toned birds fly and perch in its lush, tropical habitat. Other Bird House inhabitants include numerous endangered species, such as the Bali mynah, the Guam rail (extinct in the wild), and a variety of Hawaiian birds. Outdoor enclosures provide tranquil space for flamingos, assorted cranes, cassowaries, and other large species.

American Prairie, located along Olmsted Walk, opened in July 1999. Two bison, a prairie-dog colony, and plants native to the Great Plains introduce the prairie's delicate ecological system. Reflecting the prairie theme, the bison shelter recalls the Great Plain's early sod-roofed barns.

The Elephant House, with indoor and outdoor exhibit areas, is home to Asian elephants, Masai giraffes, greater one-horned Asiatic rhinoceroses, and Nile and pygmy hippopotamuses. When the Elephant House first opened, the pygmy hippos were new to the zoo world, and the National Zoo was the first to breed the species in captivity. A descendant of the original pair is still in the National Zoo's collection. The building, completed in 1937, is decorated with twelve relief panels of cast aluminum and five terrazzo medallions set in the floor, all depicting prehistoric mammals. Charles R. Knight, an artist closely associated with the Public Works of Art Project and other Depression-era government relief programs, designed these decorative elements as well as the stone bas-reliefs over the building's entrances.

At the Reptile Discovery Center, families with school-age children can explore the biology of reptiles and amphibians. Visitors may use listening, visual, and olfactory skills to investigate how "herptiles" feed and communicate. Afterward, families can apply their knowledge to

living animals, which include alligator turtles, king cobras, tentacled snakes, alligators, gavials, and Komodo dragons. The Reptile Discovery Center is located in the former Reptile House. Fantastical carved reptiles, sculpted doors, and columns at its main entrance decorate the facade of this Romanesque building which, when it opened in 1931, was recognized by the American Institute of Architects as the outstanding brick building in eastern United States.

In the Invertebrate Exhibit, the diverse, but often ignored, world of animals without backbones comes to life. Insects, sponges, sea stars, mollusks, crabs, and other invertebrates—the creatures that make up the vast majority of living things—are stunningly exhibited in ways that allow for close-up study. In an adjoining glass-enclosed addition, the Pollinarium with blooming plants, butterflies, and hummingbirds illus-

**Top: The Nile hippopotamus, whose eyes and nostrils are located near the top of its head, can submerge itself in water and almost completely disguise its presence. Bottom: A pair of highly endangered Asian rhinos lives at the Zoo's Elephant House.**

trates the evolution, beauty, and mechanics of animals' role in plant reproduction.

The theme at the Think Tank, formerly the Monkey House and the Zoo's oldest animal building, helps visitors understand the process of thinking in animals. Orangutans and macaques are able to demonstrate cognitive skills as visitors watch. Orangutans can also move between the Think Tank and their Great Ape House enclosures, several hundred feet farther along Olmsted Walk, by swinging, or brachiating, across the Orangutan Transport System. This series of towers connected by heavy cables allows orangutans to move as they would in their heavily forested, tropical homes.

Great Cats is home territory for some of the Zoo's favorite animals: lions and tigers. Other highlights of the exhibit include Tiger Tracks, a 250-foot-long educational trail lined with displays comparing life in a tiger family to family interactions among humans. The Predator's Alcove, a 500-square-foot museum-style display, showcases spectacular sharp-toothed fossils and explains the ecology of large carnivores.

A walk through Amazonia introduces visitors to the high degree of biological diversity in a tropical rainforest. This forest habitat, with a meandering stream, is home to a diverse array of free-ranging amphibians, mammals, and birds. Schools of exotic fish swim in huge aquariums that visitors can see from the exhibit's lower level before they ascend to the upper level's forest habitat. Smaller aquariums and terrariums in a replication of a biologist's tropical field station give visitors a chance for closer inspection and perhaps even interaction with Amazonia's staff of animal keepers.

In Amazonia Science Gallery, a working science facility, visitors have access to labs and scientists working on nutrition, molecular genetics, animal behavior,

**Top: Several of the National Zoo's orangutans participate in a computer-based language project at Think Tank. Bottom: The National Zoo's gorilla family gives visitors insights into the great ape's behavior and social structure. Opposite: Sumatran tigers, extremely rare in the wild, are being bred at the National Zoo.**

and geographic information systems. Changing exhibits, interactive computer programs, art, and books beckon visitors to take some time to explore a natural history topic that has piqued their interest.

The Visitors Center, near the Connecticut Avenue entrance, has an auditorium, a bookstore, restrooms, and an interactive learning center. "How Do You Zoo?" (open Saturdays and Sundays from 10 A.M. to 4 P.M.) gives children between the ages of 5 and 10 the chance to role play as a zookeeper, veterinarian, or nutritionist. Regular lectures take place in the auditorium and are free to the public. The lectures, featuring scientists and authors of books about natural history, are broadcast on the National Zoo's Web site. Free notifications for lecture broadcasts are available; send your request by e-mail to rsvp@nzp.si.edu.

The National Zoo's cheetah Conservation Station allows visitors to see this endangered cat in a naturalistic habitat that encourages behavior typical to that observed in the wild.

## CONSERVATION AND RESEARCH

What the visitor sees at the National Zoo reveals only a small part of its complexity as a scientific research organization. The "hidden" Zoo is internationally known as a place where scientists pursue conservation and research programs in animal behavior, ecology, and propagation. At the animal hospital and scientific research building on the Zoo grounds—and at the 3,150-acre Conservation and Research Center—zoologists, veterinarians, and reproductive physiologists study wild animal ecology and behavior in efforts to improve the care of animals and facilitate their breeding. Zoo scientists at the Conservation and Research Center, 75 miles west of Washington, D.C., in the foothills of the Blue Ridge Mountains, focus on five areas: population recovery of endangered species, reproductive biology, genome re-

source banking, veterinary medicine, and the application of geographic information systems for conservation purposes. Researchers there also conduct studies in the field, both in the United States and around the globe, and provide on-site training for wildlife professionals in developing countries.

## HISTORY

Although the Smithsonian Institution received gifts of live animals almost from its beginning, there was no zoo to house and study the living collection. Some of the animals were sent to zoos elsewhere; some were kept on the National Mall. Over the years, a sizable menagerie accumulated outside the Smithsonian Castle. In 1889, Congress established the National Zoological Park at the urging of Samuel Pierpont Langley, third Secretary of the Smithsonian, and William T. Hornaday, a

Above: The Zoo's red kangaroos are among the largest of Australia's kangaroo species. Opposite: Orange julia butterflies can be seen in the Zoo's Pollinarium exhibit.

Smithsonian naturalist who was particularly concerned about the looming extinction of the American bison. Six bison were among the animals transferred from the Mall to the National Zoo when the grounds opened in 1891.

Animal collecting expeditions in the early 1900s, together with gifts from individuals and foreign governments and exchanges with other zoos, augmented the Zoo's population and introduced Washingtonians to rare and exotic animals, including the Tasmanian wolf (now extinct), bongo, and Komodo dragon.

Today, the National Zoo continues to develop a bond between humans and animals that helps the public understand biology and scientific concepts that will guide them in making informed choices in daily life. Exhibits, educational programs, school programs, training opportunities, and public lectures all bring the rich diversity of life on Earth to a variety of local, national, and international audiences. As the Zoo moves into the 21st century, its mission is to study, celebrate, and help protect the diversity of animals and natural habitats.

## FRIENDS OF THE NATIONAL ZOO

Friends of the National Zoo (FONZ) is a nonprofit membership organization of families and individuals who participate in special Zoo programs; promote the goals of the National Zoo in conservation, education, and research; and support the fund-raising objectives of the director. FONZ volunteers serve as Zoo guides, help in animal behavior studies, receive wildlife publications, and participate in special events. Proceeds from the concessions operated by FONZ are used to advance Zoo education and research programs.

The Zoo is three blocks from the Woodley Park/Zoo/Adams Morgan Metrorail station and is accessible by Metrobus. For Metro information, call 202-637-7000, or 202-638-3780 (TTY), or check the Web site wmata.com. Limited pay parking is available on Zoo lots. Bus-passenger discharge and pickup and limited free bus parking are available.

## HOURS (unless otherwise posted)

Summer (May 1–September 15): Grounds open 6 A.M. to 8 P.M.; buildings open 10 A.M. to 6 P.M. Winter (September 16–April 30): Grounds open 6 A.M. to 6 P.M.; buildings open 10 A.M. to 4:30 P.M.

## TOURS

Guided weekend tours of Zoo highlights for families, individuals, or groups are available with an eight-week advance reservation. Call Friends of the National Zoo at 202-673-4956 or send an e-mail to tours@fonz.org.

## SERVICES

The Zoo has ramped building entrances and restroom facilities for nonambulatory visitors. Strollers may be rented in season for a small fee. A limited number of wheelchairs is available to borrow. Zoo police provide lost-and-found service and a refuge for lost children.

## WHERE TO EAT

The Zoo has a variety of fast-food facilities. Picnic areas are located throughout the grounds, but no outdoor cooking is permitted.

## GIFT SHOPS AND BOOKSTORE

Unique zoo-oriented articles—souvenirs, postcards, books, T-shirts, and art objects—are for sale.

## FEEDING TIMES

Check at the information desks for feeding times and demonstrations.

## HELPFUL HINTS

Consider using public transportation. Zoo parking lots often fill up early in the warm months. Wear comfortable clothing  and shoes. Do not overexert in hot weather; rest in the shade. During the warmer months, visit early in the day or in the evening, when the park is less crowded and the animals are more active. Fall and early winter are great times to visit the Zoo.

## SOME RULES TO FOLLOW

Pets, except certified assistance animals, are not permitted in the park. The area between the guardrail and the enclosure barrier is for your safety and that of the animals. Stay on your side of the guardrail. Zoo animals are wild and easily excited. Do not feed or attempt to touch the animals. The Zoo provides excellent, balanced diets, and additional feeding is unhealthy for them. Do not skate or ride bicycles in the park. Radios and tape players must be used with earphones.

Above: Wallpaper, René Crevel (French), ca. 1920. Opposite top: "Atomic" clock, George Nelson Associates, 1949. Opposite bottom: Back view of the Cooper-Hewitt, National Design Museum.

## COOPER-HEWITT, NATIONAL DESIGN MUSEUM

2 East 91st Street
(at Fifth Avenue),
New York City.
Open Tuesday, 10 A.M.
to 9 P.M.; Wednesday
through Saturday,
10 A.M. to 5 P.M.;
Sunday, 12 noon
to 5 P.M.
(closed Mondays and
federal holidays).
Admission charged.
Information:
212-849-8400.
www.si.edu/ndm

Cooper-Hewitt, National Design Museum is the only museum in the nation devoted exclusively to historic and contemporary design. The museum embraces fields as varied as architecture; industrial, landscape, interior, and graphic design; textiles; and fashion. With the conviction that design touches everyone, every day, in the spaces in which they live and work, the objects they use, and the messages they read and send, the museum presents compelling perspectives on the impact of design through dynamic exhibitions, educational programs, and publications.

Cooper-Hewitt was founded in 1897 by Amy, Eleanor, and Sarah Hewitt—granddaughters of industrialist Peter Cooper. A branch of the Smithsonian since 1967, the museum is housed in the magnificent Andrew Carnegie mansion on Fifth Avenue in New York City.

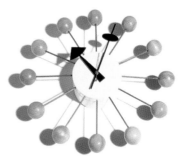

## EXHIBITIONS

Cooper-Hewitt's galleries are devoted to changing exhibitions that examine design as it relates to daily life. The museum stimulates thought about the various aspects of design—from the look of a product to practical questions of function—with presentations ranging from domestic artifacts to contemporary digital media. Exhibitions look at cultural patterns in design history and address environmental and social concerns as they affect and are affected by design. In addition to the following shows, rotating selections from the museum's collection are on display in the Nancy and Edwin Marks Collections Gallery. This special gallery features exhibitions that explore the question "What Is Design?" and are curated by museum staff and notable guest curators.

### "SKIN: SURFACE, SUBSTANCE, AND DESIGN"

*Spring 2002*

Skin is the outer surface of a person or product. It is the frontier of physical contact from person to person, and from person to the built environment. Enhanced and simulated "skins" are found throughout contemporary design, as designers subtly manipulate the relationship between the inside and the outside of products, garments, and buildings, creating skins that both reveal and conceal. This exhibition juxtaposes an international mix of products, fashion, furniture, architecture, and digital media to explore the role of skin as outer surface and structural form.

**Barcelona chair, model #90, Ludwig Mies van der Rohe (German), 1929.**

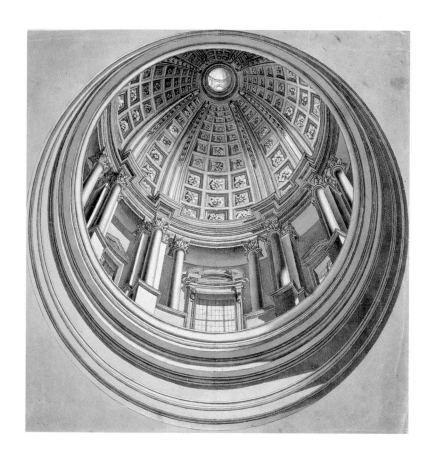

## "NEW HOTELS FOR GLOBAL NOMADS"

*Winter 2002–3*

As tourism and travel have become synonymous with many people's social and economic life-styles, hotels have transformed into the crossroads of our connected, nomadic society. Featuring full-scale custom installations commissioned by the museum, models, drawings, and photographs, as well as products such as furnishings, toiletries, and souvenirs, this exhibition highlights a new generation of international hotels that respond to remarkable growth in travel for business and pleasure.

## NATIONAL DESIGN TRIENNIAL 2003

*Spring 2003*

Launched to critical acclaim in 2000, the Triennial presents architecture; interior, product, and graphic

*Perspective Design for a Painted Cupola of a Church*, after Andrea Pozzo (Italian), 1700–1725.

design; and new media from across the country that demonstrate the impulses, issues, and ideas driving contemporary design in the United States. The only exhibition of its kind in the United States, the Triennial features the work of approximately 100 designers, focusing on emerging talent as well as a selection of mature leaders.

Top: Furnishing fabric, produced by Favre, France, early 19th century. Bottom: Matchsafe with tinder cord, Russia, late 19th century. Opposite top: *Feathers*, Alexander Girard (American), 1957. Opposite bottom: Chair, Charles Eames (American), 1944.

## COLLECTIONS

With more than 250,000 objects spanning more than 2,000 years, Cooper-Hewitt is one of the largest repositories of design in the world. Its collections are international in scope and date from the Han dynasty to the present. It has impressive holdings of furniture, metalwork, glass, ceramics, jewelry, woodwork, embroidery, woven and printed textiles, lace, and wallcoverings. The museum also

As the Smithsonian's showcase for design, the Cooper-Hewitt, National Design Museum presents changing exhibitions of historic and contemporary design. The museum promotes "good design," fosters a better understanding of the design process, and examines the influence objects and spaces have on our daily lives. Visitors can tour the exhibitions and the building—the landmark Andrew Carnegie mansion on Museum Mile in New York City—and enjoy the Arthur Ross Terrace and Garden, one of the city's only large private gardens, and, by appointment, research the unparalleled collections.

has one of the largest collections of drawings in the United States, a large collection of prints—including examples of architectural drawings, advertising, and fashion, theater, and interior design—and an important specialized library. The collections are organized in four curatorial departments—Applied Arts and Industrial Design, Drawings and Prints, Textiles, and Wallcoverings—and are supported by design archives and a reference library with more than 60,000 volumes, including 5,000 rare books.

Since its founding, Cooper-Hewitt has served as a visual library, dedicated to the purpose of improving the quality of life through design. Whether in the galleries or by appointment for private study, its collections and resources are available to everyone.

## INFORMATION DESK

Just inside the main entrance

## TOURS

Guided tours are available for groups of six or more by advance arrangement with the Education Department; call 212-849-8380. Free gallery talks are scheduled for current exhibitions.

## MUSEUM STORE

The museum store, located near the main entrance, offers exhibition catalogues; posters; slides; postcards; books on the decorative arts, architecture, and design; books relating to the museum's collections and current exhibitions; jewelry; ceramics; and gift items.

## CAFÉ

The café—in the Agnes Bourne Bridge Gallery and Lester and Enid Morse Garden Room year-round, and extending into the Arthur Ross Terrace and Garden in warm-weather months—serves a full selection of sandwiches, pastries, chips, cold beverages, and tea and coffee.

## EDUCATIONAL PROGRAMS

The museum has an active calendar of workshops, courses, lectures, study tours, and seminars throughout the year, including programs for all ages and the entire family. Free summer concerts take place in the Arthur Ross Terrace and Garden. Special children's programs are available for school groups. With Parsons School of Design and The Smithsonian Associates, Cooper-Hewitt offers a two-year program leading to a master of arts degree in the history of decorative arts.

## RESEARCH FACILITIES

The museum's library contains more than 60,000 volumes, including 5,000 rare books. The library's picture collections include material on color, pattern, textiles, symbols, advertising, and interior and industrial design. It also has graphic and industrial design archives. Object study centers are available for textiles, drawings and prints, and wallcoverings. The research facilities are open by appointment; call 212-849-8400.

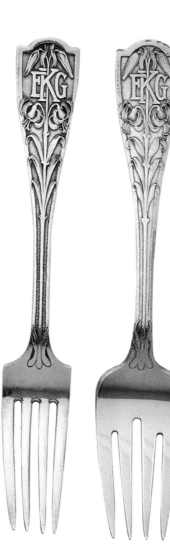

Above: Silver flatware,
George Washington
Maher (American), 1912.
Opposite: *Ladies' Old
Fashioned Shoes,* Plate
IX, T. Watson Greig,
Edinburgh, Scotland,
1885.

Above: Mapuche poncho
(detail), early 20th cen-
tury, Chile. Mrs. Thea
Heye-Lothrop Expedition.

# NATIONAL MUSEUM OF THE AMERICAN INDIAN, GEORGE GUSTAV HEYE CENTER

The National Museum of the American Indian is an institution of living cultures dedicated to the preservation, study, and exhibition of the life, languages, literature, history, and arts of the Native peoples of the Americas. Established by an act of Congress in 1989, the museum works in collaboration with Native peoples of the Western Hemisphere, including the Hawaiian Islands, to protect and foster their cultures by reaffirming traditions and beliefs, encouraging contemporary artistic expression, and providing a forum for Native voices.

The museum is made up of three facilities: the George Gustav Heye Center in New York City, the Cultural Resources Center in Suitland, Maryland, and the museum on the National Mall in Washington, D.C., scheduled to open in 2004.

*In New York City:*
Alexander Hamilton
U.S. Custom House,
One Bowling Green
(accessible entrance:
sidewalk level, corner
of Bowling Green and
State Street).
Open daily, except
December 25, 10 A.M.
to 5 P.M., Thursdays
until 8 P.M.
Admission is free.
Recorded information:
212-668-6624.
Membership
information:
1-800-242-6624.
AmericanIndian.si.edu

*In Washington, D.C.:*
Welcome Center on the
National Mall
(on the construction
site of the museum
that will open in 2004):
Independence Avenue
between 3rd and 4th
Streets, SW.
Open Monday
through Saturday
10 A.M. to 4 P.M.

## AT A GLANCE

Spanning the Western Hemisphere from the Arctic Circle to Tierra del Fuego, the collections of the National Museum of the American Indian are among the finest and most comprehensive assemblages of Native cultural materials in the world. The museum's George Gustav Heye Center was conceived as a place where the indigenous peoples of the Americas can celebrate their cultural heritage and share with scholars and visitors some aspects of what it means to be Indian.

All three facilities have been designed in consultation with Native communities. The Heye Center, described in this guide, is a permanent exhibition and education facility that presents permanent and temporary exhibitions as well as music and dance programs, films, and symposia.

The Cultural Resources Center in Suitland is home to the museum's collections and serves as a research center for Native and non-Native scholars. It contains a resource center, conservation laboratories, a library, and curatorial offices. In keeping with the museum's commitment to its Native constituencies, the center shares its vast human and material resources throughout the hemisphere and the world.

The National Museum of the American Indian will open in 2004 on the National Mall in Washington, D.C., on a site between the National Air and Space Museum and the U.S. Capitol. It will be a monument to living cultures, hosting ceremonies, public programs, and educational activities, and will provide exhibition space for Indian arts and material culture.

## COLLECTIONS

The collections of the former Museum of the American Indian, Heye Foundation, are the cornerstone of the national museum. Assembled largely by New Yorker George Gustav Heye (1874–1957), they span more than 10,000 years of Native heritage, from ancient stone Clovis points to modern silkscreen prints.

Among the thousands of masterworks are intricate wood, horn, and stone carvings from the Northwest Coast of North America; elegantly painted hides and garments from the North American Plains; pottery and basketry from the southwestern

United States; ceramic figures from the Caribbean; jade beautifully carved by the Olmec and Maya peoples; textiles and gold offerings made by Andean cultures; elaborate featherwork by the peoples of Amazonia; and paintings by contemporary Native American artists. About 70 percent of the more than 800,000 objects represent cultures in the United States and Canada; 30 percent represent cultures in Mexico and Central and South America.

The collections include materials not only of cultural, historical, and aesthetic interest but also of spiritual significance. Contemporary Native peoples of the Western Hemisphere draw on their connection to an-

Above: Larry Beck (Yup'ik, 1938–1994), *Ooger uk inua* (Walrus Spirit), 1982. Indian Arts and Crafts Board Collection, Department of the Interior, at the National Museum of the American Indian. Opposite: Mohawk beaded pincushion, ca. 1900, Caughnawaga, Quebec.

cient traditions and ways of being to survive in a vastly changed cultural landscape. Out of respect for this sense of cultural continuum, funerary, religious, and ceremonial objects associated with living cultures are displayed only with the approval of the appropriate tribe. Upon request, the museum will return human remains and funerary objects, religious and ceremonial artifacts, or communally owned tribal property to individual descendants or tribal groups who can demonstrate a cultural affiliation and factual claim to the property in question.

**Cecilia Fire Thunder (Oglala Lakota), pair of dolls, late 20th century.**

## EXHIBITIONS

The George Gustav Heye Center presents diverse exhibitions, ranging from explorations of historical cultural materials from the museum's vast collections to traveling exhibitions of contemporary Native artistic expressions. **"SPIRIT CAPTURE: NATIVE AMERICANS AND THE PHOTOGRAPHIC IMAGE,"** featuring nearly 200 works from the National Museum of the American Indian's vast archive of 125,000 images, will be on view through July 21, 2002.

**"THE NEW OLD WORLD,"** an original exhibition of approximately 70 photographs, reiterates the cultural continuance of the indigenous peoples from the Greater Antilles, including areas in Puerto Rico and the Dominican Republic, and the Lesser Antilles, where indigenous Carib communities are found in the islands of Dominica and Trinidad. It will be on view through June 2002.

**"GREAT MASTERS OF MEXICAN FOLK ART"** includes more than 800 masterworks from all 31 states of the Mexican Republic, offering a comprehensive view of the most exceptional contemporary and traditional arts of Mexico. This traveling exhibition is organized and sponsored by the Fomento Cultural Banamex A.C. based in Mexico City and will be on view from June 2002 through March 2003.

## THE HEYE CENTER BUILDING

The Alexander Hamilton U.S. Custom House, one of the most splendid Beaux-Arts buildings in New York, is rich in architectural and historic significance. It is a National Historic Landmark, listed on the National Register of Historic Places.

Blackfeet hide shirt with quillwork, mid-19th century, Montana.

Above: Model of the
National Museum of
the American Indian.
Watercolor rendering
by Elizabeth Day.

## WELCOME CENTER OF THE MUSEUM ON THE MALL

The National Museum of the American Indian Welcome Center is located on the museum's construction site on Independence Avenue between 3rd and 4th Streets, SW. The Welcome Center offers visitors an opportunity to study the museum's design, view the construction in progress, and learn about the development of the exhibitions and programs planned for the museum's opening. It features a small exhibition about the design and construction of the museum with architectural models, architectural finish boards, stunning graphic panels, and a full-scale model of a section of the copper screen wall, which will partially encircle the Potomac, the soaring central space of the museum. A computer will be available to the public to allow visitors access to the museum's Web site and other Native American resources available on the In-

ternet. The rear wall of the Welcome Center has a window overlooking the construction site where visitors can view the construction of the project. Staff will assist visitors and answer questions.

The museum on the National Mall was designed by a consortium of leading Native American and American architectural firms to blend into the Mall's urban yet parklike setting, while still retaining Native values. The flowing, curvilinear building—to be clad in magnificent natural kasota limestone from Minnesota—suggests a sculptural form shaped by wind and water. Its dome, representative of circular shapes in many Native cultures, complements the domed neoclassical buildings nearby.

Above: Hattie Tom (Chiricahua Apache), ca. 1899. Photograph by Frank A. Rinehart, Omaha, Nebraska. Opposite bottom: Lucy Parker Telles (Yosemite Miwok–Mono Lake Paiute, 1870–1956), basket, ca. 1920, Yosemite National Park, California.

## HOW TO GET THERE

The Heye Center is located on the first
and second floors of the historic
Alexander Hamilton U.S. Custom House
near Battery Park in lower Manhattan. It
is directly across from the Bowling
Green station of the East Side IRT
(trains 4 and 5) and adjacent to the
Whitehall Street station of the BMT
(trains N and R). The Broad Street
station (trains J and Z) is nearby.

### INFORMATION DESKS

In the Great Hall of the Custom House,
on the second floor across from the
main museum entrance

### EDUCATIONAL PROGRAMS

In-depth, activity-based educational programs for school groups are conducted
at the Heye Center. Native American museum staff members guide and direct

teachers as they lead their students
through hands-on learning experiences.
Reservations for these popular
programs are required and should be
made well in advance. For more information, including how to register, call
212-514-3705.

### PUBLIC PROGRAMS

The Heye Center regularly offers free
public programs showcasing the art,
culture, and lifeways of Native peoples.
Weekdays at 2 P.M. cultural interpreters lead an informal public discus-
sion in the galleries. Reservations are
not required. On selected weekends
throughout the year, the "Native American Expressive Culture" series highlights music, dance, media arts, visual
arts, theater, storytelling, and lectures. For a calendar of events, call
212-514-3888.

### RESOURCE CENTER

The Resource Center is located on the
second floor, off the Great Hall near
the main entrance to the Heye Center.

Staff is available to help orient visitors to the museum's offerings. Visitors can do research in the reference library or use the latest computer technology to learn more about Native life and history.

## FILM AND VIDEO

Films and videos by Native media makers are shown daily in the Video Viewing Room on the second floor. Staff offers information to cultural

## MUSEUM AND GALLERY SHOPS

Two shops offer discounts to National Museum of the American Indian Charter Members and Smithsonian Associates. The Gallery Shop, featuring books and unique, handmade Indian jewelry and textiles, is located on the second floor near the main entrance. The museum store, with gifts, books, and toys related to Native American culture, is on the first floor.

organizations, Native communities, educators, and the public. The Film and Video Center houses a study collection of recent works by independent and Native American filmmakers, as well as films produced by Canada's National Film Board and Mexico's Instituto Nacional Indigenista.

Above: The granddaughter of Peter Paul (Mi'kmaq), 1930, Merigomish Island, Nova Scotia, Canada. Photograph by Frederick Johnson. Opposite top: David Rubin (Inuit), painted triptych (detail), Paulatuk, Northwest Territories, Canada. Opposite bottom: Maya polychrome vase, A.D. 550–850, Nebaj, Guatemala.

## SMITHSONIAN ACROSS AMERICA

The Smithsonian's commitment to reach Americans beyond Washington, D.C., has never been stronger. New collaborations are taking shape between the Smithsonian and museums, cultural and educational organizations, and communities across the nation. More of our collections are being seen in cities and towns from coast to coast, and everywhere the focus is on expanding how the Smithsonian engages the interests and involvement of the American public. The Smithsonian's Office of National Programs offers a variety of programs, traveling exhibits, educational workshops, and partnership opportunities, all of which can be tailored and combined to meet the needs of organizations and communities across America. The four National Program units working together to achieve this national outreach mission are described on the following pages.

Above: The Smithsonian Associates study tours bring participants to America's scenic treasures, such as California's Mojave Desert. Photo © Robert Nansen. Preceding pages: Study tours offer opportunities for exploring America's diverse cultural heritage as exemplified by the Ponce Carnival celebration in Puerto Rico. Photo courtesy Puerto Rico Convention and Visitor's Bureau.

## THE SMITHSONIAN ASSOCIATES

The Smithsonian Associates offers a variety of educational programs and study tours that involve the public in the life of the Smithsonian. The Smithsonian Associates creates educational opportunities that take many forms and occur in many settings—on the National Mall, across the country, and around the world. The "Voices of Discovery" program takes outstanding scholars from the Smithsonian's research and curatorial staff into schools, museums, libraries, senior citizen and youth groups, and civic organizations to conduct inspiring presentations for students, educators, and the public. "Voices of Discovery" includes a combination of hands-on classroom activities, large group presentations, and workshops for teachers as well as public presentations and performances. Smithsonian Study Tours takes visitors, accompanied by expert guides and

well-planned itineraries, to the scenic wonders and cultural crossroads around America and the world. In addition, The Smithsonian Associates offers Washington-Baltimore–region residents a broad array of lectures, performing arts events, workshops, and seminars for all ages through the Resident Associate Program.

**Call 202-357-3030 or visit SmithsonianAssociates.org.**

## SMITHSONIAN INSTITUTION AFFILIATIONS PROGRAM

Smithsonian Affiliations is a major new outreach effort designed to share the Smithsonian's collections with the American people through partnerships with museums, science centers, and cultural institutions across the country. Affiliations are long-term relationships between partnering organizations and the Smithsonian Institution; artifacts from the national

Senator John Warner and Representative James Moran join Smithsonian Secretary Lawrence M. Small and James Rees, executive director of George Washington's Mount Vernon Estate and Gardens, in announcing a Smithsonian Affiliation.

collections are loaned for a period of up to 10 years, allowing numerous opportunities for exhibitions, educational programs, and national collaborations. The Affiliations Program also creates internship and fellowship opportunities for area students and museum staff across the country, forms national alliances with diverse cultural communities, and assists affiliate organizations through collaborative marketing and membership programs.

**Call 202-633-9157 or visit affiliations.si.edu.**

## SMITHSONIAN CENTER FOR EDUCATION AND MUSEUM STUDIES

Smithsonian Center for Education and Museum Studies links the Smithsonian's resources and expertise to the nation's classrooms through staff development and publications. Smithsonian educators offer seminars and workshops on such topics as literacy activi-

**Students create an exhibit using Smithsonian-based learning techniques.**

ties in museums, exhibition strategies for the classroom, the scientific method as it is applied to art, and the role museums can play in conflict resolution. Related publications disseminate methods and techniques to a wide audience. For museum staff members, the center provides training in diversity leadership, collections management, and Web-site development for small organizations. The center has

also taken a leadership role in making the Web a true tool for interactive learning and serves as a national gateway for children, families, and educators.

**Call 202-357-2425 or visit scemsweb.si.edu.**

## THE SMITHSONIAN INSTITUTION TRAVELING EXHIBITION SERVICE

Each year, the Smithsonian Institution Traveling Exhibition Service (SITES) shares the wealth of Smithsonian collections and research programs with millions of people outside of Washington, D.C. SITES makes available a wide range of exhibitions about art, science, and history, which are shown not only in museums but also wherever people live, work, and play: in libraries, science centers, historical societies, community centers, botanical gardens, schools, and shopping malls. Since 1952, SITES has connected Americans to their shared cultural heritage. Exhibition descriptions and tour schedules are available on the Web.

**Call 202-357-3168 or visit www.si.edu/sites.**

Traveling exhibitions such as SITES' "Earth 2U, Exploring Geography" bring the Smithsonian experience to communities around the country. Photo © National Geographic Society.

# SMITHSONIAN INSTITUTION MEMBERSHIPS

The Smithsonian invites people of all ages across the country and around the world to become Associate members. You may choose from an exciting array of membership programs. The benefits of each membership program are described below.

## NATIONAL ASSOCIATE MEMBERSHIP

*For members nationwide and worldwide, open to all.*

**SMITHSONIAN MAGAZINE (12 ISSUES).** Illuminates an exciting world of learning in the arts, sciences, and history

**STUDY TOURS AND SEMINARS.** Eligibility for travel programs with U.S. and international study tours and seminars

**ASSOCIATE AMENITIES IN WASHINGTON, D.C.** A cordial welcome and special information materials at the Associates' reception desks in the Smithsonian Institution Building (the Castle) and the National Air and Space Museum

**SMITHSONIAN REGIONAL EVENTS.** Invitations to special events occurring in your metropolitan area

**COOPER-HEWITT, NATIONAL DESIGN MUSEUM.** Free admission to the Smithsonian's National Design Museum in New York City

**DISCOUNTS** on most items purchased from the Smithsonian Institution Press, from the Smithsonian mail-order catalogue, and at Smithsonian museum stores in Washington, D.C. (excluding the National Zoo and the separately administered National Gallery of Art)

- A 10-percent discount at the Ice Cream Parlor in the National Museum of American History, Behring Center
- Reduced rates on National Museum of the American Indian membership, *The Wilson Quarterly,* and *Muse,* a children's magazine.

For more information, call 1-800-766-2149.

## RESIDENT ASSOCIATE MEMBERSHIP

*For Washington metropolitan-area residents, membership includes all National Associate benefits, plus:*

**ASSOCIATE,** a monthly publication with details about current programs and events

**FREE** lectures, tours, and family programs.

**DISCOUNTS,** as much as 35 percent, on courses, workshops, lectures, films, seminars, performing arts events, and many more activities; an additional 10 percent for all members age 60 and over.

The rich spectacle of Kunqu, traditional Chinese musical drama combining elements of theater, opera, poetry, and music, presented by the Resident Associate Program.

- With a valid membership card, a 10-percent discount in the Commons, a 19th-century dining room in the Smithsonian Castle, and preferential reservations. Open Mondays through Saturdays for lunch and Sundays for brunch. Reservations recommended. Call 202-786-1229 (voice); 202-357-2957 (recording).
- Discounts on original works of art by well-known American artists commissioned by The Smithsonian Associates.

For more information, call 202-357-3030.

## CONTRIBUTING MEMBERSHIP

*Contributing Membership, available in several membership levels, offers the opportunity to help shape the Smithsonian's collection, preservation, education, and research efforts through philanthropic support. Membership privileges for those who join at the Donor level and above include all National and Resident Associate benefits, plus:*

**COMPLIMENTARY GIFT EDITIONS** of current Smithsonian publications, exhibition catalogues, recordings, and the popular *Smithsonian* engagement calendar

**RESEARCH REPORTS,** a quarterly newsletter featuring news on Smithsonian research activities

**SMITHSONIAN TODAY** newsletter and Calendar of Events

**SPECIAL EXCLUSIVE CONTRIBUTING MEMBERSHIP BEHIND-THE-SCENES TOURS** at Smithsonian museums and regional events held in communities across the country

**CHARITABLE-GIFT TAX DEDUCTIONS** based on level of membership

For more information, call 1-800-931-3226 or 202-357-1699.

**Opposite: The Smithsonian Castle, in the heart of the nation's capital.**

## AIR & SPACE ASSOCIATE MEMBERSHIP

*For enthusiasts of aviation, space flight, and modern technology. Membership includes the following benefits:*

**AIR & SPACE/SMITHSONIAN MAGAZINE (6 ISSUES).** Chronicles and celebrates human conquest of the air and exploration of the Universe

**ASSOCIATE AMENITIES IN WASHINGTON, D.C.** A cordial welcome and special information materials at the Associates' reception desks in the Smithsonian Institution Building (the Castle) and the National Air and Space Museum

**STUDY TOURS AND SEMINARS.** Eligibility for international and U.S. study tours and seminars

**LECTURES.** Participate in free lectures at the National Air and Space Museum

**DISCOUNTS** on most items purchased from the Smithsonian Institution Press, from the Smithsonian mail-order catalogue, and at Smithsonian museum stores in Washington, D.C. (excluding the National Zoo and the separately administered National Gallery of Art).

• A 10-percent discount at the Ice Cream Parlor in the National Museum of American History, Behring Center.

**REDUCED RATES** for Langley Theater films and Einstein Planetarium shows at the National Air and Space Museum

One of 12 lunar modules built for Project Apollo, "LM2" in the National Air and Space Museum was used for drop tests in Earth's atmosphere.

For more information about Smithsonian memberships and an application form, you may contact the Membership program directly or write to:

Visitor Information and
Associates' Reception Center
Smithsonian Institution
SI Building, Room 153
Washington, D.C. 20560-0010

or call 202-357-2700 (voice), or 202-357-1729 (TTY).

E-mail: info@si.edu

Please visit our Web site, www.si.edu.

Learn about other ways of supporting the Smithsonian at www.si.edu/giving.

AMERICAN ART

*Temporarily closed for renovation*

**M** GALLERY PLACE

PORTRAIT GALLERY

**TO RENWICK GALLERY**
▼ *10-minute walk from American History*

14TH STREET

12TH STREET

10TH STREET

9TH STREET

CONSTITUTION AVENUE

AMERICAN HISTORY

NATURAL HISTORY

7TH STREET

**THE CASTLE**
*Smithsonian Information Center*

SMITHSONIAN

**M**

JEFFERSON DRIVE
RIPLEY CENTER*

FREER
GALLERY

ARTS AND
INDUSTRIES

HIRSHHORN

INDEPENDENCE AVENUE

SACKLER
GALLERY*

AFRICAN
ART*

C STREET

STREET

*indicates an entrance pavilion to an underground building. The symbol **M** indicates a Metrorail station.*